P9-AET-835

Contents

The Vestry Handbook

by Christopher L. Webber

MOREHOUSE-BARLOW
Wilton, Connecticut

Morehouse-Barlow Co., Inc.
78 Danbury Road
Wilton, Connecticut 06897

Library of Congress Cataloging-in-Publication Data

Webber, Christopher.
The vestry handbook.

Bibliography: p.
Includes index.
1. Church officers—Handbooks, manuals, etc.
I. Title.
BX5967.5.W43   1988   254   88-5160

ISBN 0-8192-1453-1 (pbk.)

Printed in the United States of America
by
BSC Litho
Harrisburg, PA

10 9 8 7 6 5 4 3 2 1

Foreword

During my years as bishop in the Diocese of Hawaii, one of the most rewarding experiences was my regular meetings with the wardens, vestries, and bishop's committees of the congregations of the diocese. There was the annual meeting with the newly elected that was an all-day orientation program for the new ministry to which these congregational leaders had been called. There were the area meetings with wardens for Bible study and personal sharing of ministry concerns.

At each of these gatherings of church leaders, the definition of the responsibilities in the ministry of the member of the vestry and bishop's committee was constantly reveiwed. For as the individuals came to understand more clearly their ministry to support, nurture, and enable the total ministry of the people of God within their congregations, the importance of their roles as leaders grew in clarity.

It would have been most helpful to have a resource as has been prepared by Father Webber to supplement existing resources that have been available to the church in the past. As the ministry of our congregations continues to address the pains of our society, so too the role and ministry of vestry members have expanded. There is an ongoing need for the education and nurturing of our leaders . . . providing them with the proper resources and knowledge that will enable them to fulfill their commitment to Christ and to their communities.

We are indebted to all who seek to assist those who follow Christ to fulfill the ministry to which they have been called. And for his efforts, Father Webber is to be commended.

Edmond L. Browning
Presiding Bishop

Introduction

This book is planned to give perspective, ideas, and resources to wardens and vestry members. No one, probably, will want to read it through like a novel. There is no plot, no character development, and no surprise ending. This book might better be used as a resource to dip into from time to time. Those asked to serve on a particular committee may find a relevant chapter. Others may find references in the index to areas that interest them. The place to begin is with the immediate assignment. Other sections, such as that on the diocese and national church, may be useful background to fill in when there is time.

Note also the suggestions that may be more properly the province of the rector. This book assumes a parish with an open style of leadership in which suggestions are always welcomed and everyone is expected to contribute. If this book suggests a new way of doing things that has some appeal, the hope is that vestry and clergy can work together in a spirit of collegiality to explore new possibilities and, where appropriate, implement them.

Read the section "Working for Change" and the section "Burnout." Try to balance idealism and realism. Be sensitive to others. Rely on prayer. God has a purpose for you and for your parish. You cannot accomplish it. This book does not have all the answers. But God's grace is always sufficient.

CHAPTER 1

The Role of a Vestry Member

Canons and Customs

The vestry of an Episcopal church has three primary responsibilities. The first two are managerial: to take care of the parish finances and parish buildings. The third responsibility (though all or part of it may be assigned to the parish meeting in some dioceses) is to choose individuals to fill various positions of parish leadership and representation: the election of a rector, the choice of delegates to the diocesan convention, and the selection of other individuals as the diocesan canons and parish bylaws may stipulate. All these responsibilities are defined by the laws of the church that are called "canons."

Beyond this, most vestries quickly find that they have a wide variety of duties ranging from the assignment of ushers at services to the making of plans for the parish's future. Some of these responsibilities may be spelled out in vestry bylaws or result from specific parish decisions. Others may simply be the result of generally accepted parish customs: "We've always done it that way."

In addition to the canons and local bylaws and customs, there are sometimes state laws that define the responsibilities of religious corporations and that may be different for each denomination. In the case of the Episcopal church, these laws may specify election procedures and even the date when the annual meeting is to be held. It might also be pointed out that, contrary to the common mythology about "separation of church and state," the clergy must conform to state law when they perform marriages, and in that role they function as officers of the state. The laws that regulate a church's operations are not, of course, intended to restrict or inhibit the church but only to provide some ultimate referee should that be necessary.

It is important for vestry members to be familiar with the laws of church and state under which they operate and to be certain that they are in conformity with them. Parishes often fall into habits that are out of keeping with these laws and thereby expose themselves to the possibility of serious problems if someone feels mistreated or if the parish becomes involved in controversy over, for example, the sale of a building or the use of its land. Such issues can become very emotional, and, if proper procedures are not followed—even in the election of the vestry members who made the decision—complex and expensive legal actions can result.

Many parishes have brought together the church's canons, the state's laws, and whatever local customs they feel are important and formally adopted them as "parish bylaws." Such a compilation can be very helpful and should be reviewed from time to time by someone with legal training and experience.

Every new member of the vestry should be provided with such a set of bylaws. Every vestry member should review the bylaws regularly and be familiar with their provisions. Copies of the diocesan canons and national canons should also be available to vestry members, perhaps in a parish library or other convenient location.

Every vestry should also, from time to time, review the responsibilities it is attempting to carry out and ask whether it is more appropriate for the vestry or some other group to deal with each assignment and, if it does seem best for the vestry to accept the responsibility, to ask whether the vestry is properly structured to perform the task.

Bylaws and structure may not be subjects of great interest to all members of the vestry, and reviewing them may seem a waste of time. But where they are neglected there is greater possibility of wasting time and creating conflict. Clear organizational lines are a first priority in getting the job done.

Narrow legalism and a concern to defend one's "turf," however, can also obstruct progress. Canons, laws, and bylaws may assign the rector, wardens, and vestry members specific roles to play or jobs to do, but none of these individuals can perform those duties adequately without the help, support, and understanding of the others. The vestry is responsible for finances, for example, but the rector's leadership will make the necessary fund-raising easier. The rector, conversely, is responsible for worship, but an informed and supportive vestry can help him or her make wise decisions and interpret them to the parish.

St. Paul's analogy of the Church as "one body with many members" is always helpful. No member can say to the others, "I have no need of you" (1 Cor. 12:21). Where those with specific responsibilities are clear as to what their duties are but open to the contribution others can make and eager to work together, the church will "make bodily growth and build itself up in love" (Eph. 4:16).

Representation, Leadership, and Communications

Vestry members are elected by the whole parish and should, of course, try to represent the interests of all parish members. It is worth noticing, however, that most parishes have some system for nominating candidates for the vestry and that a nominating committee will usually try to see that both men and women, both younger and older members, are included among the nominees. Perhaps specific parish groups, such as the Episcopal Church Women, will be represented. If vestry members are also members of other such groups within the parish, they should naturally make it a point to report to their groups either formally or informally on vestry matters. Such reporting will, in turn, enable them to bring to vestry meetings the concerns of others and to represent those concerns constructively.

Leadership, however, involves more than representation. Former Yale football coach Herman Hickman once said that he felt it was his job to keep the Yale alumni "sullen but not mutinous." Leadership is not a matter of simply reflecting other people's opinions and so keeping them happy but of learning, educating, informing, and persuading others.

Leadership involves working to realize a vision of what the parish could be but is not. It involves change. That may leave some members "sullen" but, if it is done patiently and lovingly, "mutiny" can generally be avoided. Indeed, a corporate spirit can grow that will reach into every aspect of parish life.

Leadership is a matter also of prayer and Bible study. The financial and property concerns of a vestry are not something wholly separate from the church's life of worship or its mission to serve others. The decision to paint the church will leave less money available for outreach, but failure to paint or repair the church may make the church less attractive to new members and therefore less able to support future outreach programs. Such choices are not easily made and cannot be governed only by financial considerations. Decisions not growing out of prayer and Bible study and worship will be less likely to sustain and nourish the parish as it seeks to carry out its primary mission in obedience to the Holy Spirit.

Finally, vestry members have a liaison role to play between the parish members and the clergy and staff. They should help the clergy hear members who may not be willing or able to speak for themselves and help the parish understand the work the clergy are doing and the pressures they may be under. Good communications are critically important if the members of the body are to work together and support each other in love.

CHAPTER 2

Vestry Structures:
With a Note on the Annual Meeting

The national and diocesan canons provide only minimal guidance as to parish and vestry structures: usually the rector is the presiding officer, there are two wardens, there are vestry members (though the number is not specified), and there is a senior warden who presides in the absence of the rector. Some of these matters may be specified by diocesan canons or state laws, but none of them is provided for in the national canons of the church.

Whatever guidelines and requirements do exist still leave a great deal of room for variation and flexibility in working out the details. Probably no two parishes operate in exactly the same way. What is important is that each parish, while conforming to the minimum standards that are set, finds a style that works for that parish.

If certain issues keep coming up without being resolved, if meetings tend to bog down in details and run on at great length, if some members have no sense of involvement, if there is a growing sense of frustration, perhaps the time has come to consider structuring the vestry in some new and, perhaps, more satisfactory way. There are many models from which to choose, and time spent considering modification or replacement of the existing system could, in the long run, be time well spent.

Leadership

The key to a successful vestry is undoubtedly the leadership it is given. But this is not to place the whole responsibility on the rector or wardens. Leadership (apart from personality factors) is a matter of defining issues, setting agenda, choosing individuals to carry out tasks, and keeping in touch with those to whom work is assigned to see that it is going forward. Leadership is, in large part, a matter of memos and phone calls.

It may be that the rector can do all this in addition to carrying out the pastoral and teaching ministry, but it will be better done if it is shared and, in large part, delegated. Rectors of small parishes may well be more skilled at operating a mimeograph machine than anyone else they could call on. Rectors of parishes of any size may well find it easier to carry out particular tasks themselves than to make phone calls to find someone else able to do the same work. Wardens and vestry members are subject to the same temptations. All should keep in mind a balance between efficiency and involvement. Building parish community requires involvement, and that may be destructive of efficiency to some degree. Often, however, it is worth losing efficiency to gain involvement. No one can do it all. A job worth doing is a job worth sharing.

A duly constituted executive committee, meeting at regular intervals, may be the first step toward systematic sharing of leadership. In traditional English practice, the rector and wardens *are* the vestry. The simplest executive committee might be constituted in the same way. Some parishes might wish to add two or three chairpersons of key committees. Some parishes establish the executive committee in the parish bylaws and may also give it specific authority to act between meetings of the vestry. In other parishes, the executive committee is less formally structured—simply a matter of the rector, wardens, and others getting together from time to time to see how things are going—but that runs the risk of seeming to create an "in-group" or "cabal" that runs things without specific authority to do so or any need to report.

A properly constituted executive committee, meeting at regular intervals and reporting to the vestry, can make all the difference in the way the vestry is able to carry out its work. The executive committee can appoint the leadership of other committees and each member can take responsibility for following through to see that other committees are functioning properly.

Wardens

Although an Episcopal parish usually has two wardens, there are some differences among dioceses in the way wardens are chosen and in the titles they are given. In some dioceses, one warden is elected at the annual parish meeting for a two-year term. In other dioceses, the rector appoints a "rector's warden" while the vestry elects a "people's warden." Some parishes have bylaws that specify that the vestry designates the senior warden and that person need not be "senior" in term of service. Although the canons provide only a minimal description of the wardens' responsibilities, it is almost inevitable that the wardens will play an important part not only in the vestry itself but also in setting the tone for the parish as a whole. The wardens' prayer life, pastoral instincts, and faithfulness in worship will set an example and provide leadership more important than executive ability.

The only specific duty assigned to "churchwardens" in the national canons is to notify the bishop "when a parish is without a rector," and even this duty may be carried out by "other proper officers" (III, 18, Sec. 1). Usually one of the wardens will preside in the absence of the rector, and some states and dioceses specifically provide for this. If the rector is disabled or resigns, this can, of course, become a very significant responsibility. But, for the most part, the wardens' leadership will be more a matter of tradition and chemistry. The relationships the wardens establish can bring the opportunity to exercise enormous influence. The clergy will turn to them for support and guidance; parishioners will turn to them for leadership; all will look to them as enablers and communicators whose gifts and commitment will make things happen and bring the parish together in support of common goals.

To repeat: the canons offer little guidance to the wardens as to their role. Their ministry will become effective through such ordinary means as taking the rector to lunch at regular intervals, being careful to talk to as many parishioners as possible at coffee hours and other parish events, spending time on the telephone in "follow-up," and, above all, praying daily for the parish and all its members.

Committees, Commissions, Task Forces, Parish Councils

The assigned work of the vestry is, as has been said, finances and property. Theoretically, a vestry could assign one committee to each of these areas and need no further structure. In some small parishes, the vestry may act as a "committee of the whole" with no further structure at all. The typical parish, however, will need committees of some sort to deal with everything from Christian education to evangelism. These can be organized within the vestry's structures, or these responsibilities may be given to a "parish council" that can function as a committee of the vestry or as an independent structure.

A parish council, made up of representatives of all parish organizations and open to the parish at large, can play an important role in planning and coordinating the parish calendar. It may also be given responsibilities in the areas of worship, evangelism, Christian education, and more. In the first situation, it might need to meet only a few times each year. In the latter case, it would probably meet monthly and play as significant a part in parish life as the vestry itself. In either case, it should report to the vestry regularly, and its presiding officer (who may, of course, be the rector or one of the wardens) should normally be invited to vestry meetings.

Having decided the scope of vestry activities (whether limited to property and finance or expanded to broader issues of parish life), the next question is how to allocate the work. Some parishes prefer three or four large committees with broad responsibilities, while others prefer to divide the work among a relatively large number of committees with narrowly defined roles. The first approach might be called the "commission" approach and could include one or two commissions on finance and property, a second commission on parish life, and a third commission on outreach and evangelism. These three or four commissions together would provide broad coverage for all the activities of the parish. Each of these commissions would then form committees to deal with the specific responsibilities in its area and would meet regularly to coordinate that work. The advantage of this method is the reduction in the volume of reports that need to come before the whole vestry. A possible disadvantage is that some members of the vestry may not have specific responsibilities. Each member of the vestry should, at least, be assigned to membership on one commission, and, of course, they might be given specific committees as their duty.

The committee system, conversely, may well provide a specific responsibility for each member of the vestry, but it brings with it the risk of lengthy vestry meetings if each committee is asked to report each month. In this case, it may be better to plan vestry meetings in such a way that some committees report only at regularly scheduled two- or three-month intervals.

In addition to the commissions or committees, most Vestries will, from time to time, appoint task forces (or ad hoc committees) to deal with specific issues such as, for example, vestry structure or parish bylaws or to carry out some specific short-term task.

The vestry may also invite specific individuals to meet with it. A representative of the women's group, youth group, or other parish organizations may add a valuable dimension and help provide better intraparish communications.

Officers of the vestry are normally a treasurer and clerk with assistants for each as needed. These are not necessarily members of the vestry. It will be simpler if the clerk, at least, is not a member, since it is hard to keep the minutes and participate in the meeting as well. Giving these positions to nonmembers also provides a way for two or more additional members of the parish to take part in its organizational work.

Although vestry meetings are, in principle, open to all, non-vestry members will, of course, seldom attend unless for a specific reason. It is, therefore, useful to invite the editor of the parish paper to attend meetings or to see that they have an early copy of the minutes so that parishioners can be informed about the work the vestry is doing and the state of the parish. Some parishes also post a copy of the minutes on a centrally located bulletin board so that all who wish to may be informed.

Dispatch of Business

The best structured vestry cannot operate efficiently unless members are well informed and decisions to be made are placed before them in a timely and clear-cut form. All this depends on effective committee work and a well-organized executive committee.

To begin with, there should almost certainly be a monthly mailing arriving well ahead of the next vestry meeting and containing the minutes of the last meeting, the agendas for the coming meeting, and reports from those committees that have proposals to present for action. The vestry should not be presented with proposals for major expenditures or other significant actions without prior notice and sufficient information to consider the matter in advance.

The ordinary parish is a relatively small community, and no one wants to create bad feelings. Therefore it is easy to fall into sloppy habits. No one is eager to say "You're out of order" or "Why not refer this back to the committee until it's done its homework?" It would be a good use of time to spend the first meeting of a new vestry establishing guidelines that are clear and that everyone agrees to respect. If it is agreed, for example, that no expenditure above a certain size will be approved unless all members have received a report in advance explaining the need and reporting the committee's recommendation and the reason for it, it will be difficult to present a matter for action on the spur of the moment. There may be occasions when urgent action is needed or when, for good reason, the committee work could not be completed in time. But these should be dealt with as exceptions and require a two-thirds—or even unanimous—vote to suspend the usual rules of order. Requiring adequate paperwork in advance will place an additional burden on the committee, but it will take a burden and source of discontent away from the vestry meeting itself. Proposals presented on paper can be dealt with far more objectively and with far less personal friction than proposals presented orally and without preparation. If the vestry members contract with each other to do their homework, vestry meetings will be a better experience for all concerned.

In the same way, the vestry should establish a fixed time to close the meeting as well as a fixed time to begin. It is not only a courtesy to let people know when they will be able to count on leaving, but it will also help move the meeting along if everyone is clear that it must end at a fixed time. Such a limit can, of course, be suspended by two-thirds or unanimous vote when necessary, but this will be the exception. If there always seems to be a need to suspend the closing time, the executive committee should spend some time analyzing the reasons for it. The problem is probably not volume of business but lack of adequate organization.

Compensating for such limits, there should also be time in every vestry meeting when any vestry member can express concerns that they feel need attention. A standard agenda item listed as "concerns" or "new business" and preferably scheduled early in the meeting will help avoid the feeling that everything is programmed in advance and "no one has a chance to say anything." Whether the issue is a community need to which the parish might respond or the way the ushers take up the offering, the matter can be brought up and referred to the appropriate committee. It should not be dealt with at that time unless it is simply a matter of a misunderstanding that can be resolved in a few words.

The Rector's Role

Although the rector is normally the presiding officer of the vestry, he or she may, on occasion or in some standard pattern, turn the chair over to one of the wardens. What cannot be relinquished, by definition, is the role of chief pastor in that community.

That role should also be evident in the rector's relationship with the vestry.

Morgan Dix, rector of Trinity Church, Wall Street, in the nineteenth century, is said to have spent some time at every meeting of the vestry instructing them in the Christian faith. It is certainly appropriate for the vestry to spend some part of every meeting in Bible study and prayer. The solution to all the parish's problems is, finally, in God's hands more than in the limited wisdom of the vestry. That perspective, reenforced at each meeting, is more important than any planning or structure. Nevertheless, to proceed without planning or structure is to fail to use whatever wisdom and ability God has given.

The rector can also strengthen communications within the parish by reporting to the vestry each month on ministry. The rector cannot, of course, tell who has been counseled and why, but statistics can be provided on the number of parish calls made and the number of counseling sessions held. Such information will help the vestry to respond to any comments such as "the rector never calls" by saying exactly how many calls have been made and offering to let the rector know that the individual in question would like to receive a visit. A fully informed vestry can be an enormous help in strengthening communications within the parish.

From time to time, the rector might also report at more length on the way a week in ministry is normally spent. Most vestry members have very little idea how the rector's time is used and can be more helpful to the rector and the parish if a clear picture is provided. The work of parish ministry is, by its very nature, never the same from one week to another and must be unstructured enough to enable the rector to respond to emergencies. Nevertheless, if the rector keeps a log for a few weeks of the number of hours spent each day in administration, meetings, services, counseling, calls, community and diocesan activities, study, sermon preparation, and the like and reports this to the vestry, that will enable the vestry to support that ministry more fully and communicate it more effectively to others.

A closer examination of such a report with the executive committee or some other appropriate committee may also enable the vestry to provide more help to the rector in certain areas that involve tasks other parish members could perform as well and free the rector for the particular ministry to which he or she is called.

Making Committees Work

The real work of the vestry is usually done in committees and a strong committee is a pearl of great price.

Leadership on committees will normally be chosen by the rector, one of the wardens, or the executive committee from individuals who have already served on that committee in the past or who have some special skills or training to bring to that area of parish life. The chairperson of each committee will normally be a member of the vestry, but, unless parish bylaws specify to the contrary, there will be occasions when it is appropriate for nonmembers to chair particular committees.

Enlisting Committee Members

Although some committee members may be assigned by the rector or wardens in order to be sure that all vestry members serve on at least one committee, the chair of each committee will usually be free to fill out the committee's membership. Depending on the work to be done, a committee of six to ten members will probably be the best size. More than that will leave some with little work to do; fewer than that will not provide enough diversity of skills and viewpoints.

Some people will say, "I work best with a small committee," or even, "I can take care of this better without a committee to slow me down." This may be true as a matter of fact, but it misses half the point. A committee is, of course, supposed to accomplish certain tasks, but a committee also serves a valuable function in bringing people together and giving them a role in the life of the parish. Every committee should include in its membership several individuals who have recently joined the parish or who have not previously served in any active way. Such individuals, if they contribute effectively to the committee's work, become part of the talent pool from which future vestry members can be drawn. Perhaps more important, they are made to feel that they have something to contribute and that the parish has been helped through their work. Giving people a sense of "ownership" may be almost as important as accomplishing specific tasks.

A committee of eight or ten members can, naturally, slow the process down, and not everyone will be as cooperative as the chairperson might like. But the community building and informational aspects of the process are generally worth the price. "Outsiders" and "newcomers" will gain a far deeper understanding of the life of the parish than they can ever gain by reading the parish paper or listening to the announcements on Sunday morning. And each informed person will, inevitably, share that information with others in a ripple effect, the value of which is beyond measure. Don't settle for small committees or the person who says, "I can handle that by myself." It may be the same person who also says, "Why is it always the same people who have to do all the work?"

The Committee Meeting

Having said everything above, let it also be said that committee meetings can be an enormous waste of time. So, hold them but plan them carefully. Committee meetings, like vestry meetings, should have a clear agenda and as much information as possible distributed to members in advance. At the very least, an agenda should be placed on a blackboard or on newsprint so that all are clear as to what the meeting is intended to accomplish. Like vestry meetings, committee meetings should begin with prayer and end at a fixed time. The chairperson should be sure the members all know each other and spend some time, if necessary, in getting acquainted and establishing guidelines for the committee's work.

The first committee meeting might begin by establishing an agenda for the year's work. This may, of course, be modified as the year goes on and new work is discovered and old work is completed. The committee should have its own "job description" and the members of the committee also should be clear as to what their role is to be. Some members bring particular expertise, some represent particular interest groups in the parish, some will be able to carry out particular tasks. All this should be defined (and acted on) as quickly as possible. Members who are not clear as to why they are there and who are not asked to assist in some definite way can go away frustrated.

Each committee should have a recorder who makes notes of what is done at the meeting and provides minutes to the other members. Such a detail may not seem important in a small committee, but it is easy to forget exactly what was agreed on or when particular decisions were made unless someone has written it down.

A Note on the Annual Parish Meeting

The national canons of the Episcopal church do not require an annual parish meeting or any parish meeting at all. There is no national requirement that wardens or vestry members be elected. The method of "selection" is left to the separate diocesan canons and state laws. Nonetheless, in most parishes, the annual meeting is taken for granted, though the time and format of the meeting vary widely.

There was a time when the standard seemed to be an evening meeting, often beginning with evening prayer and a parish supper. In recent years, it has become common to hold the meeting on Sunday following a parish eucharist and informal meal. Sometimes the rector's report to the meeting has taken the place of the sermon at the eucharist.

If there are state laws or diocesan canons that require that meetings be held at a particular time, the vestry should be careful to comply with those requirements. It is possible, if the required time seems inconvenient in a particular situation, to convene a meeting at the required time with the minimum quorum required and then adjourn to the preferred time.

Whatever the time and format, there are usually two essential matters to come before the annual meeting: (1) the election of wardens and vestry members and (2) reports on parish finances and business. These matters can take an hour or two or be dealt with so briefly that there is time for a guest speaker or program or for some important discussions and planning.

Elections

Depending on local regulations, the annual parish meeting may elect some or all of the wardens and vestry each year. A nominating committee can help ensure that there are candidates of varied ages, male and female, presenting different skills and interests. Not all parishes are comfortable with nominating more than one candidate for each office, apparently on the theory that a losing candidate may have hurt feelings. But elections without a choice may also leave parishioners with some vague (or concrete) feelings of frustration. A choice of candidates suggests a parish with leadership strength and with numerous individuals ready to take part. As for the chance of hurt feelings, see the comments below under "Conflict and Competition."

It is required in some places, and may be useful everywhere, to leave the polls open for at least an hour. A pre-stated period of time during which the polls are open provides opportunity for those who cannot attend the full meeting at least to cast their vote.

Reports

In many parishes, the annual meeting is the one opportunity most members have to be given a picture of the parish's finances, to ask questions, and to express opinions. A clear, printed summary of the finances is always helpful. Note that the annual meeting in most dioceses has no authority to approve a budget since the vestry has full financial responsibility.

Other oral reports should be carefully planned to emphasize areas where significant events have taken place or are being planned. A full set of reports from vestry committees and other parish groups can be printed and distributed. It is unnecessary to have all these reports read at the meeting, but they provide an invaluable summary of parish life.

Special Features

The annual meeting may also provide opportunity to challenge the parish in new ways and make it aware of the larger mission of the church. Perhaps an archdeacon or, on special occasions, a bishop, can provide information about diocesan programs of particular interest. Perhaps a visitor from overseas can provide a picture of the work of the church in some other part of the world.

Almost every parish meeting will see the retirement of a warden or vestry member who has completed a term of service. Recognition of such events is a way of saying something not only to the individual but also to the parish as a whole about the way individuals and their contributions are valued. Time spent saying "thank you" is always time well spent.

Conflict and Competition

There is a common—and mistaken—belief that conflict and competition are somehow un-Christian. Acts 15, however, presents a picture of life in the first days of the church in which conflict was taken for granted. We read of "no small dissension" and "much disputation." The Bible tells us that Paul disagreed vehemently with Peter, could not work with Mark, and used strong language about those with whom he disagreed (cf. Gal. 1:9; 2:11-14; 3:1; etc.).

Why should we assume that all Christians will always see things the same way? We are all at different stages of our journeys and inevitably will have different perspectives. Logically, the church can change and grow only as members present those perspectives and work to accomplish their own vision. A polite church in which each member always defers to the others is not one that would be likely to challenge its members to grow.

Why should we be unable to accept the fact that in an open and democratic society some ideas and some individuals will be chosen and others will not? If the secular world can live with defeat and rejection, how much more the church? But we need to have our priorities clear. If our goal is personal recognition, of course we will take it personally when we lose. But if our goal is God's kingdom, our own success or failure is irrelevant. Indeed, God can work through our failures as well as our successes. A parish where the annual meeting (as well as other events) is carefully set in this perspective should be able to choose among a variety of candidates and programs and be strengthened through the process. The trick is not to avoid conflict but to be sensitive to others and work always for reconciliation.

CHAPTER 3

Finances

Stewardship

Parish finances begin and end with stewardship. All that we have belongs to God and is entrusted to us to use for God's purposes. So, first, members of the parish give to the church in stewardship of their possessions, and, then, the vestry uses those offerings in good stewardship of what is given.

Stewardship and the Canvass

Stewardship and the "Every Member Canvass" are not the same thing. Stewardship is a way of living in which the parish and all its members should be growing all year and every year. The Every Member Canvass provides opportunity for church members to express their financial stewardship annually. The canvass gives focus to stewardship. Stewardship includes finances, but it includes the whole life of the parish as well.

Since the vestry is responsible for the parish's finances, it should provide leadership not only in finances but also in stewardship in the largest sense. Vestry members should be individuals whose way of life reflects a concern to use all God's gifts in God's service and in the service of others. Specifically, their personal stewardship should be an example to others. It is usually a mistake to elect someone to the vestry who has not already given evidence of good stewardship. Vestry members commonly become more aware of the needs of the parish in budgetary terms (and more critical of others who fail to "pay their share"), but they do not commonly learn stewardship in this way. Stewardship comes from faith, not from a knowledge of finance.

The vestry's financial responsibility does also, of course, involve a specific concern for the annual canvass. Whether the rector or wardens appoint the canvass committee, whether the chair of that committee is a vestry member or not, the canvass committee reports to the vestry, and the vestry is responsible for seeing that the canvass is properly planned and carried out.

Since there are excellent stewardship materials readily available from several sources (see Appendix 6), there is no need to duplicate that material here. The following points are intended only as a brief summary of essential matters to consider.

1. The vestry should be clearly committed to a high standard of stewardship. Stewardship is, first of all, a biblical priority. Jesus talked frequently about the right use of possessions (cf. Luke 12:42-48; 21:1-4; etc.). The Episcopal church at the General Convention of 1982 called on every member of the church to accept the "biblical tithe as the minimum standard of Christian giving." The vestry can provide leadership by formally accepting that standard, at least as a goal, for its members and by informing the parish that it has done so.

2. Stewardship should be a year-round activity. The stewardship committee should be formed immediately after a new vestry is elected, and it should meet regularly throughout the year to plan and carry out its work.

3. Stewardship giving should include not only the annual pledge but also a variety of other types of giving such as donations of time and talent, deferred giving, and bequests.

4. And, finally, the vestry must practice stewardship with the resources it is given. Money must be used carefully within the parish, and the needs of others should have a high priority. Some of the strongest language in Jesus' teaching has to do with the needs of the poor (Matt. 25:31-46) and the work of evangelism (Matt. 28:18-20). The vestry can hardly ask others to practice stewardship if it hoards all its resources for its own parish.

Parish Income

Pledge Income

Even though some parishes depend on endowment income for a substantial part of their budget, pledge income is a surer sign of financial health and, indeed, an important sign of spiritual health.

A parishioner moved to Florida and was called on by her new rector. As he was leaving, she said she would like to make a pledge. "Don't worry about it," said the rector. "We have all we need."

That rector may have known the financial needs of his parish, but he failed badly to meet the spiritual needs of his new parishioner—and, indeed, of the church. A parish with no financial needs is a parish with no sense of mission.

In addition to the ordinary box-of-envelopes system, there are companies that will mail envelopes to parishioners at regular intervals, and there are also electronic transfer systems available (see Appendix 6). The vestry may want to consider whether one of these systems would be helpful to a significant number of parishioners and make it available to them.

The vestry should monitor pledge income at regular intervals but limit access to individual pledge records so as to maintain their confidential nature. Many parishes send quarterly statements to pledging members. Such statements can help pledgers avoid getting too far behind as well as provide them with a record of their pledge payments for income tax purposes. The normal parish will rely on pledge income for support of most, if not all, of its local program and outreach.

Special Gifts

In addition to pledge income, most parishes will receive occasional gifts from nonpledging parishioners and additional gifts from pledgers. These can be treated as regular income but should be kept separate from pledges since no commitment has been made. Estimates of such income for budget purposes can, of course, be made on the basis of experience but it must be realized that such income cannot be relied on.

Loose Offerings

Money placed in the plate on Sunday morning but not placed in envelopes or made in fulfillment of a pledge is the "loose offering." Where this amount is relatively large or seems to be growing, it may reflect a failure in the stewardship program. If all parishioners are canvassed and newcomers are given pledge cards and envelopes promptly, the loose offering should remain a small part of the total offering.

The canons of the Episcopal church (III, 15, Sec. 2[e]) provide that the loose offering from one eucharist each month shall be given to the rector for charitable purposes. Since this amount may be small and unreliable, many rectors and vestries make an agreement that the rector will be given a set amount at regular intervals for the same purpose and in lieu of the loose offering.

Endowment Income

Some Episcopal churches are supported almost entirely by endowment income, while others have little or no income of this sort. Some parishes with substantial endowments have established foundations as a means of using their income to respond to the larger needs of the church. There is an association of endowed Episcopal churches that meets regularly to consider the special problems and opportunities of parishes with particularly large endowments (Appendix 6).

Every parish should have a program to encourage members to include the church when they make their wills. The Prayer Book directs the clergy to instruct members of the parish on their duty to make wills and "if they are able, to leave bequests for religious and charitable uses" (p. 445). Since tax laws and other legal requirements are a highly specialized area, the vestry should see that legal assistance is available to parishioners for that purpose. A simple brochure outlining the ways in which members can include the church in their estate planning can be very helpful.

It should be noted that a tithe of salary is not a full tithe since most people also own assets—a home, for example—that appreciate in value over the years. This, too, should be tithed, and the simplest way to do that is to remember the church in your will.

The canons of the Episcopal church establish very specific guidelines for the investing and recording of endowment gifts (I, 7, Sec. 1[1][2]). Every parish should, of course, comply with these requirements. Endowments must be properly recorded and properly invested. The income and principal must be held or used in accordance with the donor's instructions.

"Rental" Income

In recent years there has been a dramatic increase in the use of parish buildings by outside organizations. Some organizations are given the use of space in parish buildings as part of the parish's outreach program and as a service to the community. Other organizations make donations to the parish as a reimbursement to the parish of the cost of heat and light and janitorial services. Still other organizations enter into formal rental agreements with the host parish.

While the use of parish buildings by other nonprofit organizations can be a substantial service to the community and a welcome source of additional income, the vestry should be careful to avoid insurance liability it is not prepared to cover and tax liability on otherwise tax-exempt buildings. Insurance coverage for child-care programs has escalated rapidly in cost in recent years, and some parishes have been unable to continue such programs as a result. As parish income from use of buildings has grown, tax authorities have begin to examine such income and ask why it should not be taxed. Vestries ought to anticipate such problems and, where there is any question about the implications of a proposed "rental" arrangement, consult a lawyer or local tax authorities in advance.

The Annual Report and Audit

In addition to the vestry's regular review of the parish's financial situation, an annual report is required by the national church. This report is filed with the diocesan office, which, in turn, passes on to the national church the information needed for its records and planning. This annual report is also often used by the diocese as the basis for an "assessment," or "quota," that each parish pays to support the program, staff, and mission work of the church at the diocesan and national level.

Because the vestry is handling money given by church members as an act of stewardship, the Episcopal church requires that proper records be kept and annually reviewed by an auditor. The canon on this subject is entitled "Of Business Methods in Church Affairs" (I, 7), and the title makes clear what the objective is. An annual audit of the church's financial records must be made by a Certified Public Accountant, a Licensed Public Accountant, or an audit committee authorized by the proper diocesan authority. The audit, of course, also protects the treasurer and is a means of keeping track of the handling of funds. It is helpful to have an audit committee to review the audit or to make it a special item of business at the next meeting of the finance committee.

Treasurers and custodians of church funds exceeding $500 a year must also be bonded. Often the diocese itself provides blanket coverage for parish officers and organizations.

All these provisions are a reflection of the church's concern for good stewardship. All possessions are a sacred trust, and the church should set an example in the careful, responsible use of the money and property with which it has been entrusted by its members past and present.

The Official Accounting Manual

There is a loose leaf notebook called *A Manual of Accounting*

Principles and Reporting Practices that is available from the executive council of the Episcopal church (Appendix 6). This manual provides a history and overview of financial reporting practices for Episcopal parishes and missions. It then gives detailed information on the way a parish treasurer's books should be set up for the sake of simplicity and accuracy. Sample spread sheets and other useful reporting forms are also provided in an introductory packet. The diocesan office may be able to provide further help to a parish interested in setting up its books properly.

The Budget Process

Some parishes make a point of conducting the annual canvass first and only then constructing the budget for the next year. They reason that the budget should reflect the stewardship of the parish's members and not be simply a matter of paying bills.

A budget should, indeed, reflect stewardship, and the vestry may well postpone making a final budget until after the canvass is over. But budget making is, nonetheless, a yearlong process. There are "fixed" items in the budget that may be affected by reviews and decisions made earlier in the year. New initiatives may be made possible by the canvass, but planning for the standard budget items should not be left until after the last pledge card is returned. In fact, if planning is delayed, whatever new initiatives may be made possible by the canvass would be needlessly delayed by lack of preparation.

The emphasis in pre-canvass budget planning should be on the so-called fixed items, determining where costs can be reduced and economies realized and gathering the information that will make it possible to complete the budget quickly when the canvass is over.

Diocesan Assessment

One of the largest "fixed" items in the budget is probably the diocesan assessment, or quota. In most dioceses, this is based on parish income or some combination of parish income and membership. Usually this assessment will provide for the operating expenses of the diocese as well as its outreach and mission programs. The assessment also includes the diocesan share of the operating expenses of the national church and its mission work in this country and overseas. The assessment quota may be voluntary or compulsory depending on diocesan canons.

Whether the diocesan assessment is voluntary or compulsory, it should be a primary obligation in making the parish budget. The basic unit of the Episcopal church is the diocese, not the parish. Episcopalians are members of a worldwide church, not merely a local congregation. Wherever they go, they are immediately recognized as members with only a "letter of transfer" required to establish themselves fully in a new parish. In many Protestant churches, on the other hand, membership is in a local congregation, and members must join a new local congregation and be received by the pastor whenever they move. Thus, Episcopalians have a fundamental obligation to support the work of the diocese and, through it, the whole church of which they are members. This is also the primary means Episcopalians have of supporting the mission of the church and its outreach to those in need and those who have not yet heard the gospel.

In some dioceses, there is a two-track system that establishes an assessment for the diocesan administration budget and a separate quota for mission. Sometimes the former is obligatory and the latter is voluntary. Yet the mission quota in such a case is, if anything, the more important since it alone enables church members to carry out the gospel mandate toward others.

However the diocesan assessment is structured, it should occupy a central place in the budget process.

Salaries and Other Compensation

The largest expense area in most parish budgets will be for salaries and such related items as pension, life insurance, medical insurance, and travel. Many dioceses have adopted minimum standards in all or most of these areas. Some dioceses have rather elaborate statements that provide guidance on compensation standards in relation to years of service, size of parish, and continuing education. These standards will be discussed in more detail in chapter 6. Clearly, the salaries paid in any parish should at least meet the minimum diocesan standards and keep pace with inflation.

The best time to review salaries may be in the spring or at some remove from the annual canvass so that they do not become a mere reflection of the parish's financial situation. The staff's performance may, of course, have a direct impact on the parish's finances—but also, it may not. The death or transfer of a parishioner with a large pledge, the closing of a factory, or the passage of new tax laws may have more to do with the result of the canvass than the quality of the rector's sermons or the music program. Desirable salary levels can more easily be considered without the immediate pressures of the canvass or budget making. If adjustments must later be made in the light of canvass returns, that is understandable. But goals that cannot be met do still provide recognition and are valuable for that reason alone.

If adjustments in salaries are made after the budget is set, it will, of course, be necessary to budget a reserve line for salary increases from which adjustments may later be made.

Adjustments to salaries involve adjustments in other compensation items as well. The Church Pension Fund, for example, assesses each parish an amount based on clergy salaries. The diocese often sets a minimum standard for insurance coverage based on salary. Social Security, worker's compensation, and pension for other staff members will also depend on salary levels.

If a housing allowance is provided, this should be reviewed annually. Provision for continuing education would also come in this area.

Although some dioceses have begun to provide standards for salaries of other staff members, there is still very little guidance generally available. The American Guild of Organists (see Appendix 6) does provide guidelines for salaries and compensation, but many organists are employed on such a part-time basis that the standards are difficult to apply.

The very lack of guidelines, however, places an additional burden of responsibility on the vestry. All too often, churches take advantage of lay employees. Everyone knows that churches do not pay well. There are some compensations for that, such as a more relaxed attitude toward the scheduling of days off and a greater flexibility in scheduling work to be done. But that relaxed and flexible attitude can also translate into poorer standards of performance. If the vestry wants the church staff to perform well, it must treat the staff in a professional manner. Adequate compensation, including pensions, health insurance, and related items must be given careful annual review.

Buildings and Grounds

The second largest item in the budget will almost certainly be for the maintenance of the buildings and grounds. Under that general heading will come routine maintenance and, probably, utilities and insurance. Custodial services may be placed here or under salaries. Major repairs may be included in the annual budget or dealt with separately through special funding.

"Routine maintenance" is, of course, a matter of definition. The replacement of a roof will be a routine matter in one sense— every twenty-five or thirty years—but even if such obvious major repairs are listed separately, it is still not easy to draw the line. This is the kind of area where advance planning is important. If a careful study of the buildings has been made, it should be possible to say whether maintenance work is keeping up or falling behind and budget accordingly.

Some vestries budget for major repairs either with a line item for that purpose or through some kind of reserve fund. Since the frequency and cost of such items are almost completely unpredictable, it may be better to assume that such items will be dealt with through a capital funds campaign at regular intervals (see below).

Utilities, once a relatively minor item in the budget, have become in recent years a dominant factor in the whole pattern of life in many parishes. Under the impact of rising fuel prices, many parishes in the colder parts of the country abandoned their church buildings in midwinter and began to worship in a more easily heated parish hall or undercroft. Some are still doing it.

While gas prices are set by large utilities and regulated, oil prices can vary significantly. In some areas, group purchase plans make lower prices available. Some dealers are willing to give churches a lower price for the sake of "community relations." Price, of course, is not the only factor to consider. Reliability of supply and service must also be taken into account.

Here, too, planning ahead can be helpful. Not only can the vestry study alternative fuels and suppliers, but there is also the possibility of reducing fuel costs through further investment in insulation, through creation of separate heating zones in buildings, and through the use of automatic thermostats and timers. All of these measures are a part of the vestry's stewardship of the parish's resources.

Insurance

Insurance, also, has suddenly emerged as a major factor in church budgets as liability coverage has become exorbitant or even unavailable and insurance of all types has escalated in cost. Vestries should confer with other churches in their area to learn from their experience and consult diocesan staff for comparative information and guidance. Groups using the buildings may need to be called on for assistance in meeting these rising costs since providing space to community groups, however worthy, can no longer be done at relatively little expense. Certain "high risk" groups, such as a counseling center or nursery program, should normally provide their own insurance.

Every church should be sure that the contents of buildings as well as the buildings themselves are properly insured (see chapter 5). The varieties of insurance coverage available should be carefully reviewed to be sure that the church is not exposed to the possibility of catastrophic and irreplaceable loss. A complete inventory and professional appraisal will be valuable means toward that end.

Health and life insurance are also significant areas of expense in which various choices are available. Group plans and health maintenance organizations (HMOs) are among the options that may help to provide the needed coverage at a saving to the budget.

Other Areas

Each parish will have its own special budget items and ways of grouping related areas. Among those items that will appear in most budgets are the Christian education program, the music program, and worship. Committees responsible for those areas of parish life should be asked for a statement of their needs for the coming year and, where major increases are requested, for a justification. The budget committee may wish to schedule "hearings" to allow these groups or representatives of them to explain their hopes and plans.

Capital Funds

Every parish will have need of major funds from time to time to replace a roof, renovate a heating system, install new equipment, or cope with the aftermath of fire or flood. Some of these needs can be foreseen and some will be defrayed, in part at least, by insurance. But other such needs will, inevitably, arise without warning. A reserve fund or endowment may, of course, be available. But, whether such funds are available or not, a capital funds campaign may be the best response.

Few parishes, no matter how diligent the stewardship teaching, ever come close to realizing their giving potential. Professional fund-raisers will suggest as a rule of thumb that a capital campaign can raise three to five times the amount pledged annually over a three- to five-year period. Thus, a parish with pledge income of $100,000 might be able to raise an additional $300,000 to $500,000 in this way. Experience also shows that such a campaign will not lower the amount pledged in the ordinary canvass but will, if anything, increase it even if the special campaign is conducted at the same time as the annual canvass. A capital campaign can also direct special attention to bequests and deferred giving. And a capital campaign, by identifying special needs and projects, may appeal to some individuals in a way that the normal stewardship campaign, unfortunately, does not.

Every vestry, in its financial planning, ought therefore to consider its needs, immediate and long range, for major funding and confer with diocesan stewardship leaders or professional counsel as to the advisability of such a campaign. If such a campaign has not been conducted within the last five to ten years, it may be an important resource to investigate.

CHAPTER 4

Buildings and Grounds

The second major area of vestry responsibility is the maintenance of the buildings and other property belonging to the parish. Typically, there will be a church building, a parish hall, and a rectory. Some parishes will have additional buildings, and most will have grounds around the buildings to maintain even if it is only the sidewalk outside the church in the center of a major city. The furnishings and other contents of the buildings are also normally included in this area of concern.

Use of the Buildings

While the vestry is charged with the duty of maintaining the buildings belonging to the parish, the rector is given the use of them "for the purposes of his ministry" (canon III, 15, Sec. 1[c]). The symbolic giving of the keys in the service for the Celebration of a New Ministry signifies that the rector, on his or her own authority, may decide who may use the buildings and when. The rector is given this authority to ensure that he or she is able to conduct services, provide an educational program, and reach out to the community without hindrance. Nonetheless, in a healthy rector and vestry relationship there will be consultation and cooperative planning to avoid unnecessary divisions and to gain the broadest possible support for new programs.

The increased use of parish buildings by community groups, already referred to, creates both opportunity and challenge. Members of various groups using church buildings often begin to feel that it is "their" church. Some may well begin to attend services, and others will speak warmly of the church to others who, in turn, may begin to attend. Whether this happens or not, however, the use of church buildings to serve the community and its needs is a significant way of fulfilling the gospel mandate to serve others.

The problems of liability insurance and rental arrangements

have already been discussed (in chapter 3). Other problems, especially for a committee concerned with buildings and grounds, will be the increased wear and tear on the buildings and the increased demands made on custodial staff. Sometimes a parish begins to feel that its sexton or janitor is now working more for outside groups than for the parish. This, too, of course, can be a ministry to the community, but it needs to be the result of a considered policy that recognizes and evaluates both the value of the programs and their cost.

One way of dealing with these problems is to create a separate committee or even a semi-independent board to be responsible for community programs. Where significant outside funding is involved (or where the parish itself is supporting outside groups through special funds), this may be almost essential. Such an arrangement may make it possible to allocate costs of heat and light, insurance, and custodial services fairly between the parish and the "outside" organizations and programs. It may also help avoid a distorted picture of parish finances.

Sometimes when such an arrangement is made, the vestry itself functions in both capacities: as vestry and also as, for example, "community center board." Other parishes create a board on which the vestry is represented but that also includes wide community participation. Care should be exercised in the creation of such a committee or board that the church's interests are properly represented.

It is important to bear in mind that parish property cannot be sold or mortgaged without the consent of the bishop and standing committee, so the vestry must retain ultimate control of the church's buildings (canon I, 7, Sec. 4).

Since diocesan assessments are generally based on parish income, it may also be important to segregate funds that the church receives for community programs. Donations and "rentals" that help meet parish expenses should be treated as parish income, but governmental funds, foundation grants, and other funds intended, for example, to operate an after-school tutoring program, should be treated separately. An appropriate portion may go to the parish for maintenance and administrative costs (and so be included with receipts on which assessment will be due), but the portion used for the special programs should not be included in the base from which the diocesan assessment is reckoned.

Maintenance and renovation of buildings becomes a much

more complicated matter when several groups are using the same space at different times. Furnishings that are needed by one group may simply be in the way of another. In allowing multiple uses of space, it must be made clear to all groups, in parish and out, that they cannot simply furnish a space for their convenience. All changes in furnishings must be referred to the property committee or some other appropriate authority.

Scheduling, also, becomes a much more intricate matter as users of the parish buildings multiply. Normally, this should be handled through an established planning process, but the property committee needs to be part of that process in order to be sure that their concerns are properly considered. Planning committees may not be as aware as the property committee of, for example, the limits to which a custodial staff can be pushed. A late program one evening cannot be followed by a breakfast meeting the next morning in the same space unless there is enough custodial staff (or parish volunteers) to clear away the debris of the first event and set things in place for the second—and do it, perhaps, in the small hours of the morning.

Taking Inventory

Maintenance Agenda

The first task of a newly appointed property committee should be the development (or updating) of a list of needed repairs and maintenance. The whole committee should walk through every room and hallway of the church's buildings and make a list of rooms needing paint, tiles needing to be replaced, faucets that drip, and all the other obvious maintenance items. Some members of the committee will be seeing some parts of the buildings for the first time. It is one thing to sit in a dimly lit church at Christmastime watching your son or granddaughter in a pageant and another to shine a flashlight into an obscure corner to study cracks in the plaster.

The committee should make a room-by-room list of work to be done and then establish priorities (see Appendix 2). Individuals or subcommittees can then be assigned the task of getting estimates where needed or simply getting jobs done. Some parishes have individuals willing to contribute skills to complete minor (or even major) maintenance tasks. Other parishes find that a "volunteer work day" can accomplish a good deal—and build a sense of community while doing it.

Safety Inspection

After the committee has made the inventory of work needed, it may be useful to ask the local authorities to conduct their own safety and fire inspection of the buildings. Are fire extinguishers of the proper type, properly located, and recently inspected? Are exits properly marked and clear of impediments? Do outside doors have "panic bars" for emergency use? Are stage curtains fireproof? Are flammable materials properly stored? These, and many other questions, can best be answered by an official inspection. Note that local authorities sometimes have a way of overlooking churches and being tolerant of violations in their buildings as an expression of good will. This is no favor to the church and its members. Careful inspections, regularly made, and prompt action to correct violations are better stewardship than any expenditure on insurance policies.

Other inspections that should be made regularly are of the roofs and heating system. The church may, in fact, have contracts to see that the heating system is regularly inspected and serviced and may also have a contract with a roofer to clean gutters regularly and inspect the roofs. Preventive maintenance is always less expensive than deferred maintenance.

Major Repairs and Capital Improvements

Major repairs are generally less predictable than routine maintenance needs, but contracts such as those suggested above for regular inspection may help. The diocese or local government may be able to suggest persons who make such inspections and who can make recommendations but who, not being contractors, have no financial stake in the advice they give.

Roofs are usually guaranteed for extended periods of time. The committee should find out when the roofs were last inspected and repaired or replaced and what guarantees are operative. Roofers can tell you the "life expectancy" of the various materials used in roofing and so provide some guidance as to when replacements may be needed.

When major repairs or new buildings are needed, the diocese may have low-cost loans available. The Episcopal Church Building Fund also has funds available for parishes that qualify (see Appendix 6).

Protection

If insurance policies are part of the building committee's responsibility, these, too, should be reviewed annually to see that all buildings are properly covered. The various aspects of this problem are discussed in chapter five.

Burglaries have become a common occurrence in churches in many parts of the country. The property committee should inspect locks and security arrangements and consider the value of an alarm system. The local police department will probably be willing to make such an inspection with the committee to check the church's security and to make suggestions for improvements.

Grounds

The appearance of the church grounds can play a larger role in the church's life than most members realize. Those who are "insiders" may be totally unaware of the church's physical appearance. Their mental picture of the church, shaped by years of deep involvement, may have very little relationship to the actual picture presented to "outsiders" or newcomers. For the latter, an uneven sidewalk, a rusting sign, or a bit of litter on the church steps may dominate their picture and prevent them from coming inside at all. Committee members should stand on the sidewalk outside the church and try to see it as if for the first time. They may see things that speak more powerfully to new-comers than the best evangelism committee—and to the opposite effect.

Safety, again, must be a primary consideration of the property committee when they consider the church's grounds. An uneven sidewalk and steps without a railing may be grounds for legal action against the church should someone fall.

An elderly parishioner emerged from the dimly lit vestibule of the church into the glaring light of the midday sun and, while searching in her handbag for car keys, missed the first step, fell, and broke her leg. Though she was a longtime member of the church, her insurance agent persuaded her that her costs would not be fully covered unless she sued the church. Reluctantly, she did so. Fortunately for the church, the settlement was small. Since that time, the church has altered the railing to bring it within easier reach, revised the steps so the top step is wider, and stationed ushers by the door on bright days to escort parishioners out by a safer side door.

A closely related subject is "handicapped access," which is at last receiving the attention it deserves. Obstacles that existed unnoticed for years have suddenly—and rightly—begun to receive attention and be corrected. Few older churches were designed with much thought to ease of access. Long flights of stairs, narrow, heavy doors, and other such hazards were common. But with the older population increasing rapidly and many church members continuing active into their ninth and tenth decades, it is important for the church to do what it can to enable them to continue to participate.

Older members are not likely to complain about the physical arrangement of buildings they have loved and cared for over many years, nor do they want to "be a burden." They are more likely to see it as their own fault that they no longer have the energy to face the difficulties involved in coping with access problems. The church, therefore, needs to be especially alert. It is all too easy to say, "Well, I don't see anyone in church on crutches or in a wheelchair, so that can't be a problem." This is a problem that becomes visible only as it is resolved. Many communities now have committees on "handicapped access" that can provide guidance. This may be an area where modest expenditures can make a significant difference (see Appendix 6). If at all possible, put one or two handicapped people on the committee. No one else will have the same sensitivity to obstacles that they will have from personal experience.

Where the parish grounds extend beyond a stretch of sidewalk and include a lawn, a garden, a cemetery, or columbarium, the initial inventory should also include these areas. Is the lawn in good repair or does it need seeding or sod? Are the plantings attractive and properly pruned? Are there trees that have grown so large as to block one's view of the church instead of enhance it and that should therefore be pruned or removed? Are there trees with dead limbs that are a hazard and that should be removed? Such conditions arise gradually and are all too easily overlooked unless a committee studies the situation very carefully and systematically. Yet these conditions have a bearing on every aspect of the church's life from insurance protection to evangelism.

Using the Inventory

Once the property committee has completed an inventory, it can use it in several different ways. It provides, of course, the initial agenda for the committee itself, but it may also be of interest to several other committees. The finance committee, for example, will want to have such an inventory in order to make its plans.

The stewardship committee may want to give publicity to parish needs in connection with the canvass and may find that particular projects appeal to some individuals in a way that the ordinary budget or theology of stewardship does not. Stewardship of time and talent may take on new meaning for some who would be willing to help by contributing their time and skills to maintenance or gardening projects. At the least, the completed inventory should be shared with the vestry as a whole for any suggestions or comments they may have.

Keeping Records

Try to get someone on the building committee who never throws anything away. Be sure to file away with the inventory all records of repairs and improvements for the benefit of future committees. It is invaluable to be able to find out who rewired the basement or reshingled the steeple and when it was done and how. It is invaluable to have estimates of work to be done and diagrams of wiring and plumbing. All too often work has been done by volunteers or contractors who have left no record, and therefore it is impossible to revise or repair the work except by beginning again from scratch or tearing open walls to see what lies behind them. Make records and keep them. Your successors will bless your name.

Doing the Job

Once the inventory of buildings and grounds is completed, the committee's task will be to get estimates and to establish priorities. Emergency needs will establish priorities in one way and budgetary considerations in another. Some work may be beyond the scope of the budget and may lead the vestry to begin considering a capital campaign.

Once the priorities are established and the financing is in place, it remains only to get on with the work. A parish with a large custodial staff and superintendent of buildings, even one with a part-time business manager, should have little difficulty moving from the inventory and estimates to carrying out the task. The committee's task will be simply to see that the job is properly done.

In smaller parishes there may well be difficulty even in getting estimates. Someone will be needed who has time to spend on the telephone finding contractors and following up with them. Someone else will be needed who is available during the day to make sure that contractors have access to the buildings. It is poor stewardship to ask the rector to fulfill any of these roles simply because he or she seems "available." A rector who has to stay in the buildings waiting for a contractor is a rector who cannot be out making calls. The committee should include in its membership someone who may have no particular skills in building maintenance but who does have time to make phone calls and be in the buildings when that is required.

Clear guidelines should also be established by the vestry as to the committee's spending authority. It should not be necessary to return to the vestry with estimates to ask approval for every contract. The committee should be given advance approval for expenditures up to a certain amount and within the budget.

A Note on Cemeteries and Columbariums

A few churches in some parts of the country may have old cemeteries around them. If these still have space for burials, they can provide an important service to parishioners. Proceeds from the sale of cemetery plots should be set aside in a special fund to provide for the maintenance costs of the cemetery itself and, perhaps, the church grounds as well. As cemetery space is used up, it should be possible to use cemetery income to provide for the building of a columbarium in the cemetery or even inside the church building itself. If a cemetery is old and maintenance has been neglected, it may be possible to attract community support for the restoration of the cemetery since it will be of historic interest to the larger community.

Most churches no longer have space for cemeteries, but many could find space for a columbarium. A burial place for cremated remains can be established against the wall of the church or parish hall, within the church itself, in a chapel, an undercroft, or even a specially designated area of a parish hall. Sometimes a memorial garden is established in which ashes can be scattered without burial. Such facilities are not only a service to parishioners and others but may even be a source of additional income after perpetual-care funds have been established.

It is important in establishing a columbarium to provide a carefully drawn contract (see Appendix 4) specifying exactly what the church is responsible for in terms of maintenance. Funds raised in this way should also be carefully segregated and controlled so that the proper maintenance of the columbarium is assured.

CHAPTER 5

Insurance

Some General Comments

There was a time when the list of disasters against which an insurance policy holder was protected often ended with the phrase "and acts of God." But why should a church need such protection?

A modern definition of insurance tells us that "the primary function of insurance is to substitute certainty for uncertainty as regards the economic costs of disastrous events."* Since the Prayer Book asks God to "make us deeply sensible of the shortness and uncertainty of human life," this definition, too, might seem to make insurance a low priority for a vestry. Yet the very fact that Christians above all others should know the uncertainty of human life makes it logical that vestries in particular should act on that knowledge and do everything possible to provide adequate protection against the various risks to which an organization of any kind is inevitably exposed.

Adequate insurance coverage is simply a matter of good stewardship. It is also required by the national canons (I, 7, Sec. 1). There are no economic certainties in this life, but that which God has given us ought not to be needlessly risked. It should be preserved and protected to the best of our ability.

Unfortunately, however, there are many vestries that have not at all "substituted certainty for uncertainty" when it comes to the risks to which they are exposed. A careful review of those risks would be likely to find many of them completely uncovered and others so poorly covered as to leave the church's resources dangerously exposed. There are few better uses of vestry time

---

Encyclopaedia Britannica, The New Encyclopaedia Britannica, 15th Edition. William Benton, Publisher, 1943-1973 Chicago et al. Volume 9, p. 645.

and energy than a study of the insurance protection the church has and the protection it needs. Such a study may take many weeks to complete and will require very careful and persistent investigation.

The alternatives, however, are potentially disastrous. One obvious consequence, should a church building be lost, would be an insurance settlement grossly inadequate to replace it. A second very real possibility, following on the first, is legal action against the vestry and its members for "wrongful acts" because they had failed to provide adequate insurance protection.

Failure to act, in other words, can expose not only the church but also individual members of the vestry to significant personal loss.

Some Examples

Is your church properly protected? Consider the following examples.

Church A was a magnificent stone building erected in the nineteenth century to serve a comfortable suburban neighborhood. As the neighborhood changed, the congregation declined until finally it was taken over by the diocese and converted into a program center for Hispanic ministry. The church building was converted into offices and meeting rooms for programs. A small congregation began to meet in the rectory.

When a fire destroyed the church building, the diocese noted that it had insurance for $1,500,000 "actual cash value." But its hopes to build a more efficient center for the Hispanic ministry were dashed when the insurance company offered a settlement of $400,000.

In fact, the diocese was surprised to discover, the term "actual cash value" does not mean "actual cash." The term in insurance policies refers to the depreciated value of the building, and, when the building is no longer used as a church, it refers to the "actual cash value" of the building in its present state and for its existing program use. A parish hall or social center does not need three-foot-thick stone walls and gothic arches and Tiffany stained-glass windows. Therefore, a church building used for other purposes does not have the same "cash value" as it did when used as a church and does not need to be rebuilt to the same standard.

The failure of the diocese to understand (and the insurance company to explain) all this led to a long legal battle and a final compromise settlement that left the diocese no longer able to provide adequate space to carry on the planned programs.

Church B suffered a fire of suspicious origin and, though some walls remained standing, was a total loss for all practical purposes. The church was protected by a diocesan blanket policy that provided for "full replacement value." Reconstruction was estimated to cost (and did cost) nearly a million dollars. The insurance company offered only two-thirds of the money needed.

"Full replacement value" did not, unfortunately, guarantee that the church building could be replaced. Since the time when the church was built, building codes had changed, and the type of flooring and wiring used in the church were no longer permissible. The insurance company maintained that they were not obligated to pay the cost of the more expensive materials and processes now required since that would be to improve, not merely replace, the lost building.

Cases like these are not evidence of fraud or deception on the part of insurance companies so much as ignorance on the part of church authorities. Insurance companies use standard terminology, the meaning of which has been established by legal precedent. It is not difficult to find out what the insurance contract means and whether it provides adequate coverage. But no lay person in these matters should assume that all is well simply because the contract language sounds good.

Note also that insurance companies have an obligation to all their customers, not simply to the one who has had a fire or other loss. If a company has covered one hundred churches and one has a fire, a generous settlement for the one means higher rates for the ninety-nine other churches. That, in turn, means ninety-nine unsatisfied customers. The insurance company has a basic responsibility to keep rates down—even at the risk of offending one customer.

For this reason also, when a church does have a fire or significant loss, it should not necessarily accept the insurance company's first proposed settlement. The church and its insurance company are, inevitably, in an adversarial position to some degree even if the insurance company is chartered by the church itself. The insurance company cannot, and should not, offer a larger settlement than is legally required. The vestry, whose members are probably amateurs in the insurance world, needs professional assistance to be sure that its rightful claims are upheld. Lawyers and insurance adjusters are there for that reason and should be used. In none of the examples given was the insurance company's offer the final settlement. In some cases, the final settlement may be two or three times the amount first proposed.

Insurance for Buildings

The largest item in the church's insurance budget will usually be to protect its buildings against fire and other disasters. It is possible to buy insurance for each building alone and each risk alone, but that is not the economical path to follow. Most vestries will be wiser to buy "multiperil" coverage for all their buildings together. Such coverage may include protection not only against fires but also coverage against vandalism and malicious mischief and even liability claims. Broad forms of coverage may include building contents as well as the building.

There are several types of protection available. The vestry should understand clearly the advantages and disadvantages of each before making its selection. The most common choices are these:

Reproduction Cost Value

This type of policy is designed to enable the vestry to reproduce exactly the type of building that existed before the fire. It includes construction costs and architects fees. Since church buildings commonly were constructed in an era when such skills as stone carving and wood carving were available at modest cost, it is often nearly impossible for the modern congregation to re-create the building they have lost unless they have adequate insurance. But, for the same reason, this type of insurance is generally the most expensive to carry.

The vestry should be aware also that, even with this coverage, exact reproduction may be impossible or undesirable for several reasons. In the first place, if the skills or materials are no longer available, there is probably an exclusion clause in the policy, and the insurance company is not obligated to enable the church to reproduce the Tiffany windows or carved mullions that once delighted the congregation. In the second place (as in the case of "church B" above), the law may now require that buildings be constructed to other standards. An exact reproduction may be illegal, and that which the law now requires may be even more expensive than an exact reproduction. In the third place, on careful consideration, the vestry may realize that the odd nooks and crannies of the old building, for all their nostalgic charm, are neither useful nor desirable in the latter part of the twentieth century. But that which is not purchased will not be paid for. The vestry may have paid for sufficient insurance to replace every finial and crocket, but unless they rebuild those items, they will have paid for the insurance in vain. The insurance company will not repay them for that which is not rebuilt. The value of "reproduction cost value" insurance may not justify the cost.

Replacement Cash Value

This type of insurance is designed to enable the vestry to build a reasonable equivalent of what they have lost. Recognizing that the former building may literally be irreplaceable and that literal replacement may be undesirable, this kind of insurance is intended to provide what is needed to construct a substitute of similar quality and usefulness. Again, construction costs and architect's fees are included.

The concept of a "reasonable equivalent" does, of course, leave considerable room for differences of opinion. Does that include the possibility of greater costs to meet new building codes? And what room is there for negotiation of details? Can two offices be substituted for one classroom or one tall steeple for two short towers? Given some flexibility and the opportunity to think again about the buildings a parish needs, it is unlikely that anyone will want an exact duplicate. But what changes can be justified under the general heading of "reasonable equivalent?" And will the vestry be able to provide financing for changes that will not be paid for by the insurance?

As in the case of "reproduction cost value," this type of policy will not pay for building that is not done. The church or other building must be built in order to recover the full value of the insurance coverage for which the parish has paid.

Actual Cash Value

As the diocese learned in the example given earlier, "actual cash value" is not necessarily what the words may seem to imply. The cash value of a church building is probably very different from the sentimental value or even the practical value. "Actual cash value" takes into consideration the deterioration that has taken place, the use now being made of the building, and whatever obsolescence may have occurred.

Although this type of policy will probably not enable the

the vestry to replace the building they have known and loved, it may be that they have no desire to replace it. The vestry may know full well that the building is obsolete, poorly located, and in need of a good fire. In this case, they may save money by not buying all the insurance available. An "act of God" may then enable them to build a more efficient building in a better location with a more modest insurance settlement—plus the money they have saved on insurance bills over the years.

Other types of insurance range from "market value," which may be almost nothing, to "subjective value," which can be as high (and costly) as the vestry is able to go.

Contingent and Increased Costs

Building codes may not only require that a church be rebuilt in a more expensive manner to meet new standards (as explained above), they may also require that an undamaged portion of a building be demolished. Standard insurance policies do not pay for such demolition or for the replacement of sections of buildings destroyed by legal action rather than a fire or other disaster. Protection against these contingencies is available and should be carefully explored.

Named and Unnamed Perils

The vestry should take note of the fact that there are "named risk" policies for such specific perils as fire and flood, hurricane and insurrection, and "all risk" policies that cover all risks *except those specifically named.* The first type covers everything named, while the second covers everything not named. Churches in areas endangered by earthquakes, floods, or hurricanes, for example, should see that protection against such hazards is specifically included in their insurance program.

Coinsurance

Almost all insurance policies on real and personal property include a "coinsurance clause." This clause is designed to protect the insurance company against having to pay the total claim when a partial loss is sustained by a policy holder with only partial coverage. If, for example, a vestry has insured a church worth $1,000,000 for only $100,000 and a loss of $50,000 is incurred, the insurance company might have to pay the entire claim were it not for the coinsurance clause. Such a clause obligates the policy holder to keep insurance to a certain level (usually 80 or 90 percent) and obligates the insurance company to pay for a loss only in proportion to the insurance held. In the example given, the insurance company would be obligated for only a small part of the loss incurred. If the church insurance had been at the required level of 90 percent, or $900,000, the insurance company would pay the total $50,000 loss incurred.

Indirect Loss

Beyond the direct loss incurred in a fire or other disaster, there is the possibility of indirect loss as well. A business destroyed by fire might wish to protect itself against the loss of income that would result when it could no longer manufacture its product or serve its customers by taking additional insurance for that purpose. A church might likewise find its income depleted if it were unable to hold services for an extended period of time and pledges were not received. "Rental" income might also be lost if a parish hall were damaged and outside organizations were therefore unable to use church facilities. A parish day school unable to use its buildings might lose tuition income or might need to rent equivalent space. The vestry, under such circumstances, might face a badly unbalanced budget and might wish to provide additional insurance protection against such indirect losses.

Deductible

"Multiperil" policies and property insurance generally will have some "deductible" clause stating an amount that the insurance company will not cover, for example, the first $100 or $500. The higher the deductible, the lower the cost of the insurance. Since the primary concern in purchasing this type of insurance is protection against major disasters, a relatively high deductible may be a good way to save money. But if vandalism is included in the policy and the church has been subject to frequent occurrences of vandalism, a lower deductible may be necessary. Note also that some policies provide a "disappearing deductible." In losses beyond a certain amount, the deductible clause does not apply, and the church receives the full payment.

Building Contents and Fine Arts

Since a church has sometimes been described as "an altar with a roof over it," it may not be surprising to learn that "building" insurance will generally include not only roof, walls, and floor but also such permanent attachments as altars, pulpits, organs, pews, windows (stained or clear), and tower bells and clocks. Machinery serving the buildings, such as the pipe organ motor, boilers, and air conditioners, will probably be included (though loss caused by the explosion of a steam boiler or engine may be excluded and require separate coverage).

Building and contents may be included in one policy or insured separately, but the line between building and contents is not easily drawn. The vestry should examine its policies carefully to be sure not only that everything of value is insured but also that it is insured in the best way. The organ and stained glass, for example, will normally be included in building coverage, but a separate "fine arts" policy may be desirable for various reasons. If that option is chosen, the vestry should be sure that the organ and stained glass are specifically excluded from the building coverage and premiums.

Contents of a building will normally include movable furnishings such as Prayer Books and hymnals, chairs, pictures, vestments, and floor coverings. If the parish hall or offices are included, there will be mimeograph machines, copiers, computers, and typewriters, to say nothing of desks and lighting fixtures and files.

Many churches have communion vessels of great historic and sentimental value. These also are of special interest to burglars since they can easily be melted down and sold without a trace. In recent years, countless churches have been robbed of these and other objects. Adequate locks and other protection measures are, of course, indispensable, but insurance coverage of these objects must also be considered carefully.

Church C, an historic building, was destroyed by fire due, probably, to the overheating of its ancient wiring. The insurance company offered a settlement of $800,000 but finally paid over $2,000,000. What made the difference? The vestry had no current inventory of the building's contents, but spent a year and a half in the painstaking and ultimately successful effort to document every detail of its loss. Professional engineers and artisans were hired to reconstruct plans. Others were hired to sift through the memories of parishioners and the ashes of the building and so provide the necessary documentary evidence. They did have, fortunately, an inventory ten years old and the bill of sale for a recently installed organ. Though the cost of reconstruction was more than double the settlement because of changes and enlargements in the building, they realized that they were underinsured and believe the final settlement was fair. But they now know how much time and effort and cost could have been spared if they had kept their inventory up to date and documented their possessions before they were destroyed.

A complete inventory with descriptions of every object should be made at regular intervals, and copies should be on file in a safe location. Bills of sale and photographs are a valuable part of such an inventory.

If the church has computers, there should be backup tapes stored in a safe place off the church premises. Specific insurance for computer files is available.

Liabilities

Beyond the risks of loss a church is exposed to in the ownership of buildings and other property are the liability risks that arise from negligence in the use and maintenance of property and wrongful actions on the part of church officers and staff. Certainty and uncertainty are also critical factors here. In ages past, the risks of "plague, pestilence, and famine" were so great that no protection was possible or expected. A more secure age is more deeply offended when things go wrong and more likely to accuse those it holds responsible. Churches, in a secular world, are no longer immune to such reactions. Vestries will need to protect not only the church but also the staff and officers against a variety of legal actions.

Public Liability

Church buildings are generally filled with stairways, railings, candles, and other hazards. Members and visitors may trip and fall and injure themselves in a variety of ways. Their own insurance (assuming they have some) may provide primary coverage, but the church may well be asked to pay additional costs.

The church is exposed to risk not only in the use and maintenance of buildings but also when buildings are constructed or altered and in the sale or distribution of food or a variety of other products.

Motor Vehicles

A car owned by the church for clergy use is easily insured, but a bus used to transport parishioners or school children is very difficult and expensive to cover.

Cars owned by church members and used on church business

are sometimes covered by an endorsement to an "all risk" policy or through a separate policy. Such a policy will usually provide secondary coverage for expenses not met by the car owner's own insurance.

Staff and Vestry

"Directors and Officers" insurance ("D. & O." insurance) is available to protect the rector, wardens, and vestry against legal action resulting from decisions they have made or negligence in the carrying out of their responsibilities.

St. Bartholomew's Church, New York, has recently illustrated dramatically the potential for trouble in this area through its vestry's decision to tear down a landmarked parish building and replace it with an office tower. Those opposing the action have sued the vestry and threatened even to sue the diocesan standing committee for allowing the decision to go forward. Those favoring the action have made known their intention to sue the vestry should it withdraw from its decision. Either way, "D. & O." insurance would seem essential protection.

A vestry might also face legal action for discharging an employee without adequate (and provable) cause, for misinvestment of funds, or for failure to maintain the buildings properly. A vestry might use "D. & O." insurance to protect itself against charges that it had not provided adequate insurance protection!

Some corporations instruct their board members not to sit on any vestry or church board without "D. & O." coverage since the corporation itself might be exposed in the event of legal action.

As for the clergy, the idea of suing them for bad advice is a new one and follows on the rapid growth of malpractice actions in the field of medicine and psychiatry. So long as the clergy do not charge for counseling or advertise their services, they may be adequately covered under the church's "all risk" policy. Clergy who do charge or advertise would be well-advised to provide adequate and appropriate protection for themselves.

Financial

Direct theft of church funds can occur in many ways.

An older acolyte, returning to his parish after a term in prison for armed robbery, was returned to his former position at the altar. He quickly learned which offering envelopes contained the largest amounts of cash and pocketed them in his cassock after the final hymn. When the statements sent to parishioners began to show discrepancies, the acolyte was warned but not discharged and the ushers were carefully instructed to remove the offering plates from the credence table the moment the final hymn was ended.

Indeed, it is more surprising that such actions are rare than that they occur. Clergy and church members are, by nature (or grace), trusting; some would say naive. The opportunities for theft and embezzlement are plentiful.

Fidelity Bonds

It is common practice in the Episcopal church for the diocese to provide blanket coverage for all church officers, not only of the vestry, but of other church organizations. Parishes can provide additional protection at their discretion.

The Treasurer of a well-endowed parish drained the church accounts into his own over a period of time and then absconded. Rumors circulated that he had gone to Buffalo, and more surprise was expressed over his choice of asylum than his lapse in integrity.

Fidelity bonds protect the church against its own members and employees who are authorized to handle funds but lack integrity or are tempted beyond their ability to resist, perhaps as a result of personal circumstances.

Theft Insurance

Theft insurance, in general, is protection against "outsiders" or persons not in a position of trust. Distinctions are made for legal and insurance purposes between burglary, robbery, and other theft, but the church will probably be best served by a broad form of policy covering all loss of money, securities, and personal property as a result of theft or unexplained disappearance.

Life, Health, and Injury

Life Insurance

Life insurance can be used as a form of savings and to establish a pension, but its primary purpose is to enable beneficiaries to cope with the loss of one on whom they depend. Funeral expenses must be met immediately and, beyond that, there is often a difficult period of transition to a new pattern of life.

Full-time employees should normally be provided with life

insurance equal to one or two years' salary. The diocese may require such a level of coverage for clergy and may also provide a group plan at reasonable cost.

Health Insurance

Full-time employees (unless protected by a spouse's plan) should have adequate insurance protection, and part-time employees, even volunteers, may for various reasons be included in a parish or diocesan plan.

Should an employee face catastrophic illness, a church will inevitably *feel* responsible for that individual. To *act* responsibly beforehand is an intelligent act of good stewardship.

Worker's Compensation

Some states require that churches provide worker's compensation insurance. Such insurance may provide scheduled amounts for injuries suffered on the job and reimbursement of salary. Thus the church may be able, for example, to hire replacement help without incurring additional salary expense.

Since the Church Pension Fund only pays for disability when clergy have retired, the vestry should consider including clergy in the worker's compensation coverage.

Disability Insurance

Disability insurance is required in some states for protection against off-the-job injuries.

Other Kinds of Insurance

The particular program of each parish will, naturally, determine the extent and variety of its insurance needs. A parish with a camp program, a day-care program, or a school will have special insurance needs that will have to be considered. There are insurance programs available for every risk imaginable.

If the church depends on income from an outdoor sale, it is possible to be insured against the danger of rain.

If a food sale is held, it is possible to be insured against the danger of inadvertently selling contaminated food.

If the church owns a cemetery or columbarium, it is possible to be insured against vandalism.

If the church property includes valuable trees and shrubs, they can be insured against storm damage or vandalism.

If the church owns computers, it is possible to be insured against the loss of records through "computer error."

Summary

A well-designed insurance program begins with a careful assessment of the church's needs. An assessment of needs begins with an accurate appraisal of the value of the church's property. Insurance companies can help with this, or the church can call in independent appraisers. Local builders and architects may also be used to establish the replacement or reproduction cost of buildings.

Once needs and values are established the vestry can ask for bids from several insurance companies and compare the rates and coverages offered. Different types of insurance are available from different companies. It may also be possible to obtain lower rates if the church carries out a thorough safety program to reduce its risks.

It would be useful to talk to representatives of other churches in the diocese, especially those that have suffered significant losses in recent years, to ask what their experience has been with particular insurance companies.

Even after insurance is purchased, the vestry's work is not done. The best insurance program available cannot replace buildings instantly or reduce to any significant degree the trauma caused by a major fire. A program designed to identify and remove dangerous conditions or materials (asbestos, for example) in the buildings and to avoid damage and litigation before it occurs does not eliminate the need for insurance but may greatly reduce the need to call on that insurance for help.

Complete and up-to-date inventories are also critical. Everything the church owns should be recorded as fully as possible. The inventory itself (or a copy of it) should be kept in a safe place outside the church buildings.

And finally, each new vestry or the appropriate committee should review all these arrangements to see that everything is in order. No responsible vestry can afford not to have a thorough insurance program.

CHAPTER 6

The Care and Feeding of Rectors

Sharing the Work of Ministry

Rectors, like the members of other professions, come in a variety of styles. There are scholarly introverts, social activists, extroverted joiners, organizers, preachers, pastors, counselors, and people of prayer. Some have many of these gifts, while others have only a few. There are also, as in all professions, occasional misfits.

It is unlikely that any rector will have all of the gifts of the Spirit, and even the most gifted rector is not likely to have exactly the right gifts for every situation and every individual. This is fortunate. If, somehow, a parish should find itself with a priest able to provide every kind of ministry with equal skill, it would stifle the ministries of the vestry and lay members of the parish leaving them little if anything to do.

One of the most important ways vestry members can serve is to assess with the rector (and other clergy) the total ministry of the parish, identify strengths and weaknesses, and work to develop better ways of sharing the work that needs to be done. Many parishes are understaffed and clergy find themselves doing secretarial and custodial work that volunteers might be able to do as well or better. In other parishes, clergy may have particular skills that are not fully utilized because they are struggling to do work for which they have less aptitude. If vestry and clergy can analyze their ministry together and free each other for the work they do best, the parish as a whole will be strengthened.

Defining Relationships

The rector of an Episcopal church is elected by the vestry with the consent of the bishop. Once the rector is "instituted" by the bishop or the bishop's representative, a mutual contract is established that can only be ended by mutual consent. If the rector is called elsewhere, the vestry can, in theory at least, decline to accept a letter of resignation (canon III, 19, Sec. 1). If, on the other hand, the vestry is dissatisfied with the rector's ministry, they cannot unilaterally end the relationship. The canons of the church, in effect, require accommodation and team work. The alternative, occasionally experienced, is usually a long, drawn out, painful, and mutually destructive process.

It has been common practice for many years for a parish to issue a formal letter at the time a new rector is called in which the terms of that call are specified. This may be the subject of some prior negotiation between priest and parish and may, as a result, be signed by both parties. It is obviously helpful to have such understandings in writing since vestry membership changes over time and memories are not perfect.

This "letter of agreement" will usually include the starting salary, housing arrangements, and other compensation items such as those discussed below. All members of the vestry should be aware of the terms of this letter and of whatever diocesan guidelines exist for clergy compensation. The terms of this letter should be reviewed annually by a vestry committee, if not by the entire vestry, and revised appropriately.

In recent years, some clergy and parishes have attempted to go further and create a formal structure within which ministry can be systematically reviewed and relationships analyzed. The "letter of agreement" dealing primarily with compensation may become a "covenant" or even a "contract" drawn up by priest and vestry and signed by both. Such documents often specify a regular evaluation process and sometimes provide for dissolution of the relationship after a specific term of years if either party is dissatisfied.

Whatever the legal status of such a document may be, it can help clarify expectations and provide a mechanism for spotting problems before they become serious. It should be stressed that a covenant defines a mutual relationship in which both sides undertake obligations and in which each is responsible to the other. A review or evaluation of ministry under such a covenant should involve a process in which priest and vestry look together at the ministry they share, recognize accomplishments as well as faults, and attempt to remedy weaknesses by agreeing on specific measures that can again be evaluated after a specific period of time. Often a consultant, perhaps the rector of a neighboring parish or member of diocesan staff, can be very helpful in guiding this process.

Sample contracts and evaluation procedures are available from several sources (see Appendix 6). Clergy and parishes should probably consult the bishop or ministry commission of the diocese before entering into such agreements.

Compensation

Clergy compensation has a number of unique aspects that need to be understood. The fact that housing is often provided sets clergy apart from members of most professions (except the military), and there are also special aspects of the Internal Revenue Service code.

Salaries

Clergy stipends have seldom been generous. In January 1987, the Church Deployment Office listed thirty-five "openings" in the New England area with an average salary of approximately $20,600. At the same time, twenty-nine positions were listed on the West Coast with an average salary of $20,800. The Church Pension Fund adds an actual or estimated amount for utilities and adds 25 percent of that total as housing compensation (unless a higher allowance is paid) to establish the pension base. So the average salary level for pension purposes might be something over $26,000 including housing. At the same time, the Bureau of Labor Statistics reported that plumbers and pipe fitters (including apprentices) averaged $24,440 in 1986 and postal clerks averaged $24,908. The national average for all clergy was $20,592.

A study of clergy salaries by the Episcopal Church Foundation a dozen years earlier suggested that salaries are part of a triangle including stewardship and accountability. Salaries, they suggested, cannot rise unless the parish is working toward good stewardship, nor are they likely to rise where lay people do not fully understand what the priest's work is. Stewardship and accountability are both dealt with elsewhere in this book.

Few clergy enter the ministry with any illusions about the financial rewards to be expected, and few have significant private resources with which to compensate for inadequate salaries. The fact that most clergy spouses now have careers of their own may make it possible for clergy to survive more easily on low salaries, but vestries should not let that encourage them to allow salary standards to decline further. Already there are many clergy who say, "I would not be able to stay in this parish if my spouse were not earning a separate income." Should vestries learn to rely on a spouse's income to keep the rector solvent, they themselves will gradually become dependent also on the spouse's income to support the church and will be unable to think of themselves any longer as a truly self-supporting parish.

The vestry should have a committee that annually reviews salary levels. This committee should be familiar with whatever standards are set by the diocese. Salaries should at least conform to diocesan minimum standards and keep pace with the cost of living.

Social Security

The Social Security law treats the clergy as "self-employed" persons. This means that they are required to pay the Social Security tax themselves instead of paying half of it as an ordinary employee does, with the other half being paid by the employer.

For many years, the "self-employed" Social Security tax was only two-thirds of that paid by employed persons and their employers. Thus, clergy paid a higher Social Security tax than the ordinary employed person but received the same benefit. From the government's point of view, however, the tax received for clergy was much lower than that received for the ordinary employee, while the benefits were the same. Now, however, the government has "equalized" the tax on self-employed individuals so that they pay an amount equal to that contributed by employers and employees themselves. The result has been a drastic increase in the amount of Social Security tax clergy must pay. Since this tax is based not on salary alone but on salary plus the "fair rental value" of housing, it imposes an enormous burden on clergy. A priest, for example, provided a salary of $20,000 and housing valued at $10,000, must pay a Social Security tax based on the $30,000 total.

Some dioceses, therefore, have suggested that parishes should, as a matter of equity, compensate clergy for a theoretical "employer's share" of their Social Security tax. Yet even this raises problems since any such payment must be reported by the clergy as income—and also taxed. Some parishes, for this reason, pay their clergy 60 percent of the clergy Social Security tax to compensate them not only for the employer's share of the Social Security tax but also for the tax on that income.

Housing Allowance

The larger subject of clergy housing will be dealt with at the end of this chapter.

All clergy, whether the parish provides housing or a housing allowance, are able to take advantage of a special provision of the law that allows them to exclude from reportable income any money they spend toward maintaining a home *if the vestry has specifically designated part of their salary for that purpose.* Thus, whether the parish provides housing or not, the vestry should pass a resolution each year when the budget is adopted stating the amount of each priest's "housing allowance." This amount may be any reasonable part of the total salary provided. The clergy may actually exclude only that amount that they actually spend, so the resolution should establish a level somewhat larger than what might conceivably be spent. The clergy will have to keep records to justify the amount they exclude from reportable income should their return be audited.

If the parish provides a cash housing allowance in lieu of a rectory, that allowance should cover mortgage payments, taxes, utilities, and maintenance. Since the allowance may, in fact, not always cover the total cost and the priest may need to use some salary for the purpose, the vestry should always designate some of the salary also as housing allowance so that any such extra expenditures can also be excluded.

Suppose, for example, that the parish provides a salary of $20,000 and a housing allowance of $6,000, but the priest actually spends $7,000 for housing. The parish in this case should pass a resolution designating not only the $6,000 but at least $2,000 of the salary also as housing allowance so that the priest has enough leeway to spend as much as may be necessary for housing and still be able to exclude it from reportable income.

On the other hand, if the parish provides housing, it should still designate some part of the salary as housing allowance so the priest can buy a new chair, a rug, some light bulbs, a garbage can, and so on and exclude from reportable income whatever is spent in that way. So a parish that pays a salary of $20,000 and provides a rectory might designate $2,000 or $3,000 as "housing allowance." If the priest spends only $500, the reportable salary would be $19,500, but if $1,200 is spent, the reportable salary is $18,800.

This feature of the tax law, properly used, provides some relief to clergy in their struggle to cope with low salaries. The tax law makes this provision not only for clergy but also for members of the military services.

Pension

The Episcopal church created the Church Pension Fund in 1917 and was the first major church to make such provision for clergy retirement. As a result, the church provides comparatively well for its clergy and their spouses and children. An ordinary pension plan might provide a somewhat better return for an individual covered separately, but the Church Pension Fund does not really provide individual pension plans. Rather, it pools the funds it receives from parishes and provides coverage for all those who serve the church whether in wealthy parishes or in mission stations, whether in this country or abroad. The pension fund also provides relatively better benefits for bereaved spouses and children. It also establishes a minimum level of pension for those who have received the lowest salaries during their active ministry. Obviously this is not to the beneift of the better paid clergy, and there is, therefore, occasional grumbling about the Church Pension Fund. Some clergy clearly would be better off with some other arrangement. But the church requires all parishes to pay into the pension fund for all the clergy it employs so that it can provide appropriate benefits to those it deems deserving.

All parishes are required to pay into the pension fund at a rate based on the salary provided. Some dioceses provide that parishes that fall behind in their payments lose their vote in the diocesan convention, but the severest penalty falls on the individual who loses certain benefits when the pension assessment is not paid.

Clergy can retire on full pension at age 65 and must retire at age 72. Clergy may also retire at age 62 on a reduced pension. Disability benefits are also included in the pension plan.

It may also be useful to point out that there is a sense in which, though the pension may be a "salary" expense to the church, it is not part of "salary" to the priest since it never becomes an asset to the priest's estate. It is a "benefit" but cannot be willed to spouse or children.

Table 1
Pension Fund Formula
(hypothetical numbers)

1. Cash salary	$25,000
2. Social Security allowance	—
3. Utilities (actual or approximated)	4,000
4. Housing (25 percent of no. 1 to 3 above or actual amount if greater)	7,250
5. TOTAL	36,250
6. Pension fund assessment (18 percent of no. 5)	6,525

Other Benefits

Medical and Life Insurance. Most dioceses have a medical insurance plan that enables parishes to provide adequate coverage without the necessity of investigating alternative plans and establishing their own group. Group life insurance coverage is also generally required and minimum levels established.

Travel. Most parishes compensate their clergy in some way for the travel involved in their work. Some provide a specific amount of money to defray the cost of operating a car or other modes of transportation. Others simply provide a car to their clergy for their use on church business. Where an allowance is provided, the clergy are required to report it as income and must justify whatever deduction they claim for income tax purposes.

Continuing Education. It is becoming increasingly common for parishes to provide one week or more annually for "continuing education" and a sum of money for tuition and travel. "Sabbatical" arrangements are also becoming a common part of the agreement between priest and parish.

Continuing education time enables clergy to participate in seminars on subjects relevant to their ministry ranging from Bible study to counseling skills and even urban planning or rural land use. Sabbaticals can be used to take courses in a seminary or college or for private study, travel, writing, and reflection. Business people, teachers, medical personnel, and many others routinely set aside time to learn new techniques and deepen their understanding of their work. Clergy have the same need, and a parish will be many times repaid for providing such opportunities.

A Final Word

The rector of an Episcopal church is in a unique position when it comes time to discuss compensation since the rector normally presides at meetings of the board that decides what that compensation will be. Were the available resources unlimited, the position might be uniquely pleasant, but, since the resources tend to be sparse, the position can be uniquely awkward.

Who knows better than the rector the financial stringencies of the parish budget and the many ways in which the limited funds might be spent? Is it right to raise the rector's salary when the outreach budget may be declining and the paint peeling from the walls of the church school rooms? No one is likely to feel this tension more than the rector, yet the rector usually presides at the vestry meeting that sets the financial priorities.

It is no solution to suggest that the rector would be better off as a paid employee of the vestry. Some denominations do organize their affairs in that way, but it creates a radically different kind of relationship between clergy and people. The priest in an Episcopal parish is not simply a paid employee. The priest is paid so that the parish will have a priest's ministry and so that priest, vestry, and parish together can minister to the community in which they are placed. The vestry does not simply hire a priest and send the priest out to do ministry. It is a shared ministry that is being established and that is best represented when the priest shares the leadership and administrative roles with a vestry. That, in turn, may place the priest in an awkward position when remuneration is being discussed, but a caring vestry will find ways to take leadership in this respect and, through their stewardship of funds, give the priest sufficient financial security to enable him or her to go about the work of ministry free of needless concerns in this area and with a feeling of the parish's support and assistance.

A Note on Clergy Housing

Housing has been provided for the clergy from time immemorial. Until recent years, such provision was almost always the most appropriate pattern. Life expectancy was not great, retirement was rare, and few clergy, therefore, needed to provide retirement housing for themselves.

Today the situation is very different. A high percentage of the clergy do live to retirement age and for many years afterwards. There is, therefore, a need in the church today to enable the clergy to acquire the means to provide housing for themselves when their active ministry is over.

Low salaries for the clergy are often justified on the grounds that ample housing is provided for them. Rectories are often handsome and spacious buildings, and those who live in them can be grateful for what they are given. Yet no equity can be built up in such an arrangement. Clergy can reach retirement age needing to provide their own housing for the first time yet lacking any of the financial resources necessary to do this.

This is undoubtedly the first reason why so many parishes now provide a housing allowance instead of a rectory. The second reason is that rectories often, despite the best of intentions, prove to be a constant and unnecessary source of irritation in the relationship between priest and parish. Financial stringencies have already been mentioned. In addition, it is often difficult for vestries to inspect the rectory regularly without feeling that they are intruding on the privacy of the rector's family. Nor are vestry members necessarily skilled in assessing the need for building maintenance. Nor do vestry members always serve long enough to become aware of problems and be able to cope with them and solve them.

Some vestries have dealt successfully with this problem by placing in the annual budget a fixed amount for maintenance that the rector can obtain by providing bills for work done. Allowing this sum to accumulate over a five-year period enables the rector to plan also for major projects.

Vestries should remember, however, that though the rector may live in a house like theirs, the rector is seldom as motivated to work at maintaining and improving that house as they are. It doesn't belong to the rector. If the vestry is lucky, they will find they have selected a dedicated do-it-yourselfer who finds relaxation in fixing the roof in the off hours. Such a rector may lobby the vestry effectively for the necessary funds and even spend salary on it and leave the rectory much improved for the next incumbent. More likely, the vestry will have selected a rector whose chief interests are ideas and people and who simply does not notice the crumbling plaster in the basement or realize that there has been no new paint applied to the house in a generation. Most rectors also realize that there is no money available for maintenance anyway and, if the situation gets to bad, they can move. Vestries almost always put a house in shape for a new rector.

On the positive side, when clergy are enabled to buy housing in the community they serve, they may as a result become involved in new ways in community life. They, too, become taxpayers. They will begin to feel the economic consequences of community issues. They will share these "real world" problems with their parishioners rather than be insulated from them.

There are two primary considerations involved in the creation of a housing allowance. The first is to provide sufficient funds to enable the priest to buy a house. The second is to enable the parish to continue to provide clergy housing in the future.

For the priest to have an adequate allowance, the key factors are the down payment, the mortgage payments, taxes, utilities, furnishings, and maintenance. Where the parish owns a rectory, it is often suggested that the vestry can sell that house, invest the money, and use the proceeds to create the housing allowance. Such action might lead to an equation such as in table 2.

Table 2
Creation of a Housing Allowance
Resources Available

Sale of Rectory	$100,000	
Less $25,000 down payment on new house	75,000	
Investment income from balance		7,500
Formerly budgeted for utilities and maintenance		3,000
Available for housing allowance		10,500

Resources Needed

Payments on $75,000 mortgage	10,000
Property Tax	1,500
Maintenance and utilities	3,500
Furnishings	1,000
TOTAL	16,000

Should the rector be able to provide a down payment from his own funds, the full sale price of the rectory might be invested and produce a larger allowance. Such an allowance might more nearly balance the rector's needs, but it would still leave the parish with no growth in its investment in housing and, therefore, a declining ability to keep up with inflation and provide an adequate housing allowance for future rectors.

To maintain its equity and balance inflation, the vestry may need to budget an additional $5,000 to $10,000 per year.*

Thus, a vestry considering a housing allowance may find the budgetary requirement for clergy compensation increased by as much as 25 percent. Clearly such an increase in the budget would not be easy, but the vestry must weigh its own financial concerns against those of its clergy and decide whether vestry members

---

*Another factor to consider is the down payment on new housing. This can be dealt with by an agreement between vestry and rector that the vestry will make the down payment and receive in return 25 percent of the proceeds at the time of sale. In this case, (and assuming the rector maintains the house properly) the vestry will need to budget somewhat less to compensate for inflation.

have an obligation to provide adequately for those they call to serve them.

There is at least one alternative to consider. Some parishes, rather than provide a housing allowance, continue to provide a rectory, but with it they also make regular payments into an escrow account in lieu of a housing allowance. Such payments may serve the purpose of establishing a reserve account for the rector against future housing needs and enable the rector to put aside a sum equivalent to the equity that might have been gained from a housing allowance—but at less cost to the parish. This escrow account might be established on a tax-deferred basis. The other benefits of a housing allowance, however, such as removal of the rectory as an irritant in the clergy-parish relationship and involvement of the rector in local tax concerns, would be lost in this kind of arrangement.

CHAPTER 7

The Parish Staff

Every Episcopal church, no matter how small, has at least four staff positions to be filled: priest, organist, sexton, and secretary. It may be that the same one individual—the priest—fills all four positions because the budget is too small to pay for more than one person. If so, the vestry should at least realize that it has only a part-time priest and is actually paying the priest to be a part-time sexton and secretary and, possibly, even musician as well.

Many priests are willing to do the parish's secretarial work and a good deal of the custodial work in order to help balance the budget, but the vestry should see the situation as it is in order to be able to exercise good stewardship of the rector or vicar's time and talent, as well as their own.

It may be that volunteers could be enlisted to free the rector to visit and teach. It may be that a priest could serve two parishes, giving part-time to each and thus free the budget in both places to provide part-time secretarial assistance. The priest would then be able to give full-time to ministry and have adequate secretarial assistance as well. Furthermore, the budget in both parishes would be clearly allocated for the particular work to be done.

The point is that there are many possible ways to use both human and financial resources. It is all too easy for the priest to run the mimeograph machine or copier, set up chairs for a meeting, and clean out the furnace room rather than search for volunteers or other ways of getting the job done. Rather than rely on the priest to do all the odds and ends of work no one else notices, it would be better to make a careful analysis of the ministry needed and a deliberate decision as to the best use of the time, talent, and funds available.

As a parish grows, it becomes possible to hire additional staff—and also to enlist additional volunteers. A part-time organist is ordinarily the first need filled, followed shortly by a part-time sexton. Secretarial help is very commonly given by volunteers (and the rector's family) until the parish attains some size. But secretarial help is most likely of all the staff positions to free the rector for the work of ministry and enable him or her to spend more time with parishioners. It is important that people be able to reach the priest and that they know that telephones will be answered and calls returned. Answering machines, of course, are easily available and will be a useful asset in almost any parish for times when the office is closed or no one is available. But answering machines are still machines and seldom know where the rector is and when the rector will return. They can seldom answer even simple questions. A good team of volunteers may be able to fill that need, but, ironically, smaller parishes may have fewer volunteers available than larger ones that may need them less. Paid assistance even a few mornings a week may be the best investment a small parish can make to strengthen its ministry.

In short, the vestry and clergy have many options available in developing a parish staff. Individuals can be hired part-time or full-time to do one job or a combination of jobs. Paid staff can be combined with volunteers. The right "mix" will depend on such factors as the skills and preferences of clergy and vestry, the financial resources of the parish, and the availability of volunteers. A vestry committee or subcommittee should be given specific responsibility for annually reviewing staff requirements, development, and compensation.

Volunteers

Every parish, from the smallest chapel to the largest cathedral, will rely to some degree on volunteers. The use of volunteers at any level requires planning and recognition. Well-intentioned volunteers without clear job descriptions can take on too much and run the risk of creating friction if they intrude on someone else's territory. They can be frustrated if their responsibilities are left so "open" that the work to be done is either not carried out when expected or not carried out at all. Clear job descriptions are always important.

Recognition is the other critical factor in a successful volunteer program. "Thank-you's" are always in order and so is a mention in the church bulletin and annual meeting report. An annual luncheon for volunteers can be an eloquent way to express appreciation.

Volunteers are, by definition, not paid, but a coffee pot in the office, a refrigerator stocked with snacks or lunch makings, perhaps even a provided lunch for those working through the day might be a helpful budget item as "volunteer program support."

The vestry should also check its insurance policies to be certain that the church is protected for liability in any accident that might happen to volunteers on duty.

Secretarial

No staff position is likely to make so obvious a difference day by day as that of "parish secretary." There are, undoubtedly, still parishes where that position is filled, however intentionally or unintentionally, by the rector's wife. But more and more often the rector's wife is holding a full-time job outside the home. And, besides that, the rector's spouse may be male.

If the rectory is empty during the day, it can be very difficult to reach the rector, whether in a pastoral emergency or for some routine church business. A telephone answering machine in the rectory or parish office is a minimal necessity in most parishes today, but a real voice coming from someone who knows where the rector is and when the rector will return is even better.

Some parishes, as has been said, can fill this role with volunteers, and some clergy and vestries will prefer a volunteer system or have no financial alternative. For others, the dependability of a paid secretary, even part-time, who is familiar with parish procedures and can carry them out efficiently will be worth every penny it costs.

Even a parish with one or more full-time paid secretaries, however, will find many ways to use volunteers in the parish office. A volunteer to answer the telephone can reduce the interruptions that make it difficult for a paid secretary to complete a task. And there is always sorting, collating, duplicating, addressing, folding, and filing that a secretary will usually be happy to share. In most parishes there are retired men and women, young mothers, and others willing and able to lend a hand and glad of the opportunity for sociability.

Custodial

Even very small parishes will usually find that life is simpler if someone is paid to sweep the floors regularly, put out the trash, and perform other routine custodial chores. Volunteers could do all these things, but few volunteers are as reliable as a person who is paid.

The sexton (see Appendix 5) may be someone hired to come in on Saturdays to take care of the cleaning or be the supervisor of a large staff of individuals with various skills. The sexton may also have a liturgical function, doubling as the verger (see Appendix 5), who leads processions on important occasions and assists the clergy in the conduct of weddings and funerals.

Custodial work can, of course, be divided in many ways. Some parishes will have extensive grounds and hire gardeners to care for them; some will have a maintenance staff to carry out minor (or even major) repairs; some will have an engineering staff to maintain a heating plant and deal with the plumbing. Most parishes, however, will hope to find one or two individuals on a part-time or full-time basis to do as much of this as possible and hire specialists as needed to deal with the more difficult problems as they arise.

Whatever the duties assigned to the sexton, there should be a detailed and specific job description so that everyone is clear as to what is expected. It should also be made clear who is to exercise immediate supervision of the sexton since the sexton, as a member of the staff, is under the rector's direction but will also need to work with the chair or an assigned member of the property committee.

Ultimate responsibility for the condition of the church rests with the rector, but the property committee is charged with the duties of maintenance and will have authority from the vestry to expend the necessary funds. This, again, is an area where the rector-vestry relationship will work best if it is "task-oriented" rather than "turf-oriented."

Music

The position least likely to be filled adequately with a volunteer is that of organist or music director. The music of the Episcopal church has always had an exceptional reputation, and it has often been influential in the decision made by newcomers to join the church. The music, with Christian education and preaching, makes a critical first impression on visitors, and the church that wants to grow will not cut corners in this area. The hiring of an organist is, then, the second most important personnel decision any parish will make.

Under the canons of the Episcopal church, the music is under the control of the rector (II, 6, Sec. 1). The rector remains ultimately responsible for the music program no matter who may be hired to direct it. The reason this is so is that the music must be carefully integrated into the liturgy. While the organist will normally choose preludes and postludes, will probably select the anthems as well, and may even choose the hymns, all these choices should be made in consultation with the rector since it is the Bible readings and the perspective the rector takes in dealing with them in the sermon that set the theme of the day, which the music should complement and reinforce.

These considerations, in turn, make it vital that the selection of an organist rest finally with the rector. Quite apart from the fact that all key staff positions should be filled by the chief staff officer, the need for close personal collaboration between rector and organist makes it critical that it be so in this case.

On the other hand, the rector can certainly be assisted in the choice of an organist by a committee of vestry members and others, some of whom should have special training in music. There could even be value in an advisory committee of nonchurch members with particular musical skills or in having such individuals serve on or with the committee. Such a committee might screen candidates and present the rector with two or three final candidates with the requisite skills. The rector's choice could then center on the liturgical sensitivity and experience of the candidates and on personal compatibility.

Just as a rector cannot be expected to have a complete range of skills and should expect to find support from the vestry and other parishioners, so, too, the organist's work will normally be enhanced and strengthened by an active support committee. Such a committee's activities may range from the cleaning and renewal of vestments to the arranging and publicizing of special musical events. Even a paid choir will find its morale improved by an annual "choir appreciation" event, whether in the context of a Sunday service, after the Sunday service, or at a special time.

The organist's job description, especially if the position is considered to be part-time, should include not only the parish's expectations concerning services and rehearsals but also arrangements for weddings and funerals and special events. Is it expected that the organist will always be available, that the organist will arrange for substitutes, or that these services must be scheduled at times when the organist is available? It is normal practice for the parish to set fees for the organist for each such service and to ensure that the individuals requesting the services are aware of these fees and pay them. The size of these fees could be established by consultation with other similar churches in the area.

The part-time character of the organist's position in many churches should not obscure the fact that the time involved includes not only services and rehearsals but also the time required to study the liturgy, plan (and, from time to time, acquire) the appropriate music, and practice. Each hour of service and rehearsal time requires several hours of planning and practice time. Meetings with the rector, a music committee, and other parish groups will also be required in most parishes. And an organist will normally have a pastoral relationship with choir members involving telephone calls, home calls, and sometimes hospital visits. All this is part of the organist's job and should be kept in mind by the vestry and support committee in drawing a job description and establishing salary and benefit levels. Further guidance is available in a brochure published by the American Guild of Organists (see Appendix 6).

Pastoral Staff

Additional clergy should not be added to the staff without a careful analysis of the ministry to be performed and the alternative ways of carrying it out. It should be remembered that most of the administrative, youth, and Christian education work normally assigned to additional members of the clergy could be performed equally well (or better) by lay persons, if (which may not be the case) there are lay persons properly trained and available for the salary offered. Even pastoral work such as home visits and counseling may be better performed by properly trained laity. Ordination is necessary only for sacramental acts and for preaching.* Part-time assistance from retired clergy or clergy in secular positions might provide whatever assistance in these areas is needed. A full salary might then be available for a business manager or administrative assistant who could free the rector for a fuller and more effective pastoral ministry.

An analysis of ministry would include not only what the parish hopes to do but also the strengths of clergy and lay people already on the staff. The Church Deployment Office has instruments

---

*Lay persons who are competent, licensed by the bishop, and invited by the "Member of the Clergy in charge" are also permitted by the canons to preach (III, 2, Sec. 5).

available for analyzing the pastoral specialties of clergy as well as the relevant characteristics of a parish (see Appendix 6). Often the diocese will have a deployment officer available to parishes as a consultant or be able to recommend someone with such skills. The use of these resources is as important in the employment of assistant clergy as in the search for a rector.

The selection of assistant clergy is, of course, the responsibility of the rector since assistants must be able to work closely with the rector and carry out the rector's program. Nevertheless, the rector may find it helpful to form a committee to assist in the evaluation and search process.

Some parishes have traditionally seen it as part of their ministry to employ a second or third priest as a part of that priest's training. Some dioceses even subsidize such positions in qualified parishes. Parishes can contribute to the life of the church as a whole by providing such positions while themselves gaining from the insights and particular skills of a recently ordained deacon or priest.

The selection of assistant clergy must always be carried out with the knowledge, advice, and consent of the diocesan bishop.

Compensation

Working for a church often provides certain benefits that enable the vestry to obtain dedicated workers for less than competitive wages. It should be clear to all concerned what the trade-offs are. A part-time sexton, for example, may be willing to work for a relatively low salary in return for the convenience of a job near home that can be done at whatever hours are convenient. A young woman may be willing to take a job as secretary in a suburban parish with few benefits and low salary because it enables her to work in the community where her children are in school and so be readily available to respond in an emergency, to be home at lunch time, work shorter hours, and avoid commuting. A music teacher in a school or college may be happy to find a job as a church organist to supplement income. A retired accountant or banker may be willing to take a position as business manager to add variety to retirement years and supplement pension while retaining enough flexibility of hours to play golf twice a week and indulge other interests.

All of these persons may also feel that in working for the church they are, in effect, donating some of their time and skills to a worthwhile cause, indeed that they have a vocation and ministry that can be expressed in this way.

Nonetheless, the church that makes such arrangements accepts certain liabilities in so doing. Other staff members, volunteers, and vestry members will have to be flexible themselves in adjusting to various schedules and standards. Work may not always be done on time and it may be more difficult to criticize work not done well.

More important, by skimping on salaries and benefits, the vestry may convey to the staff members a message that their work (indeed, the staff member also) is not very important. The church that proclaims a caring ministry may create the impression that it does not really care about the people at the center of its own life. Such an impression can be overcome when church members work to support the staff, help them as volunteers, express appreciation for work well done, and create an atmosphere that is conducive to loyal and faithful service. It can also be overcome by vestry committee work that provides clear job descriptions, a careful annual review of performance, and salaries and benefits that are perceived as fair and that are, in fact, the highest standard the church can attain.

The vestry committee responsible for staff salaries and benefits should be sure that it meets all diocesan standards where such exist. Dioceses are increasingly setting salary and benefit standards for lay workers and providing group insurance plans that parishes can enter on behalf of their employees. A vestry committee can also find out what other comparable churches in the area, Episcopal and other, are providing for their employees and use that information for guidance.

All full-time employees should have health insurance provided (unless a spouse's employment provides adequate coverage for both) and, unless the staff members themselves agree for adequate reasons to waive the requirement, a pension plan that, with Social Security, will provide an adequate income after retirement. Pension plans should also be keyed to a definite retirement age.

It is only fair to all employees that they be aware of a time by which they will need to have their retirement plans made so that they and the vestry can plan together toward that end. A fixed retirement age also allows the vestry to avoid the awkward situations that otherwise inevitably arise in a small staff when it becomes evident that a sexton is no longer able to do the heavy work required or that an organist is beginning to lose the patience required to deal with a children's choir.

Churches, however, are not exempt from the national legislation that has outlawed a fixed retirement age. Retirement must be the result of choice or an agreement between employer and employee. It cannot be compulsory except for cause and that cause may need to be documented.

Tenure

No staff position in an Episcopal church includes tenure except that of a duly elected and "settled" rector (canon III, 18, Sec. 1-4 and canon III, 19, Sec. 1). Other staff positions may be given limited tenure, such as a five-year contract, but all such provisions are limited by the rector's tenure. When a new rector is elected, all members of the staff should offer their resignations so that the rector can select a compatible staff. Even if the staff members are talented and dedicated individuals, it is likely that they will have certain expectations developed by working with the former rector that may cause friction with the new one. A certain transition period is inevitable and some holdover period may be helpful to the new rector. But the new rector should have the option of retaining staff or not at his discretion, and all staff job descriptions and letters of agreement should make it clear that this will be the case.

CHAPTER 8

A Vision for Your Parish

A newly elected vestry needs, above anything else, to take time to reflect on its vision of the parish and its understanding of its mission. Many vestries plan an annual "overnight" or time apart to get priorities straight, perhaps with the help of a consultant and perhaps with other selected members of the parish. The diocese may have a conference center that can be used, and that is probably the ideal. But many vestries find that it is possible to "get away" very simply by borrowing space in a neighboring parish's buildings, arranging to have a group in that parish serve them lunch, and returning the favor by way of payment.

There are many ways to use such time. It can be useful even to veteran members to take the time to review financial statements carefully and ask the sort of detailed questions for which there is little time available in the monthly meeting. It can be useful to review the job descriptions of the various committees and the particular needs of the parish for which each committee is responsible. But it will be even better to spend the bulk of the time building again, with the words of the Bible as foundation, a vision of what the parish is called to be so that the work of the year can be set in that perspective. Occasionally at least, the vestry might even spend some time in a traditional "retreat" with a retreat conductor and long periods of silence and meditation. A shared ministry requires not only that the rector be familiar with the financial situation but also that the vestry be familiar with the things of the Spirit.

Setting Goals

One useful exercise to conduct in a vestry "time apart" is the establishment of a parish "statement of purpose" (see Appendix 3). Can the vestry, for example, state in one sentence—"twenty-five words or less"—the purpose that inspires parish life? The effort to arrive at such an agreed statement (and more than the traditional "twenty-five words" may well be needed) might itself be the focus of parish study over an extended period of time. The vestry's adoption of a statement of purpose might be the end result of much work and thought by many parish groups and meetings. A consultant can also be helpful in shaping a process through which all can contribute their own vision of what the parish means to them and what it might be for others.

One well-planned vestry conference might, of course, come to agreement on a very clear definition of purpose. But even if it did, that statement should still be the subject of discussion at a general parish meeting (perhaps the annual parish meeting) and other forums in the parish. The vestry may find that what was clear to them is not so obvious to others. The statement may need further revision or may require an educational process to bring about general agreement and support.

More likely the vestry itself will need time and continuing discussion, further research, prayer, and Bible study to bring the whole range of parish life into a single statement. A consultant or single member of the vestry might well be assigned to draft a statement on the basis of priorities listed by the vestry as a whole. It is usually easier for an individual to do this and then let the vestry edit and modify the result rather than expect a committee to be able to frame a single statement themselves.

Once a statement of parish purpose has been achieved, however, it becomes an invaluable tool for many purposes. Placed on the Sunday bulletin, it reminds parish members of the goals toward which they are working and, at the same time, gives newcomers evidence of a parish that has a clear sense of what it is about. Read and remembered at an annual planning meeting, it can give shape and direction to a whole year's calendar.

Goals and Objectives

Beyond the statement of parish purpose lies an opportunity to define specific goals and objectives. The statement of purpose is a broad, general statement of mission. That statement should then lead to the definition of goals that will help make that mission a reality. And finally, each unit within the parish—vestry committees, church school, women's groups, ushers, and others—should define their objectives in terms that, in one standard definition, are "specific, time-limited, achievable, and capable of evaluation."

The following examples may help to illustrate the point.

Purpose: "... to make known God's love."

Goal A: "... to bring more people into the church."

Objective 1: "... to add five new families by the end of the year."

Goal B: "... to devote more energy to serving those in need."

Objective 1: "... to participate in the community soup kitchen on a regular basis."

Objective 2: "... to see that each shut-in member of the parish is called on each month by another parishioner."

The "purpose" might be achieved in many ways and so might the "goals." The result of such general statements might be to inspire new effort, but might also, since no specific objectives are set, remain unrealized and produce only vague feelings of guilt. Clearly stated and attainable objectives, on the other hand, can produce a feeling of accomplishment and release new energies and make new accomplishments possible.

Such clear definitions also provide a standard by which to measure almost every parish activity. Does a traditional luncheon bridge serve to advance the vision? Is an annual bazaar or rummage sale a good use of energies? Perhaps such activities build a sense of community or enable the parish to support a shelter for the homeless and so contribute directly to a stated goal. If so, they can be supported with new enthusiasm. But if, on the other hand, they are being planned simply from habit, if they drain energies, create friction, and produce little in return, the vestry now has a way to put an end to it by applying an objective statement of goals to which the parish has agreed, rather than stepping on sensitive toes.

More important, the development of a statement of purpose will enable the vestry to put first things first. It is true of many churches that people go to them for the music, the program, the architecture, or the social status, but it is unlikely that any vestry or parish will identify itself in that way if challenged. Rather, a disciplined, prayerful attempt to state priorities will almost inevitably focus on the meaning of Jesus Christ as Lord of human lives. Such a focus may be expressed in many ways: in preaching, in sacraments, in ministry to others, in daily life and work. And yet if the vestry and parish are agreed in saying that Jesus Christ is the center and meaning of their common life, it will tend to become increasingly true in all

those ways. That will be the most important step forward any
vestry can take.

Spiritual Growth

If goals must be stated in realistic and measurable terms, how is
it possible to deal with the spiritual growth that is surely the
parish's fundamental reason for being? How can one measure
holiness? It is all too easy to assume that this is impossible and
therefore that the parish can simply carry on doing things as they
have always been done, hoping for the best.

In fact, however, we can probably measure spiritual progress
in about the same way as growth in most other areas of parish
life. Does increased pledging really indicate growth in stewardship
or is it merely a superficial sign? Does increased church school
attendance indicate growing knowledge of the faith or is it simply
one indication among many? So likewise, increase in the number
of communions, participation in prayer groups, attendance at
Bible study and so on may not guarantee that spiritual growth
is occurring, but it does provide some measurable evidence. Jesus
did say, "By their fruit you will know them" (Matt. 7:16).

There is no infallible way to be sure that spiritual growth is
occurring. Not everyone who begins to pray daily or study the
Bible regularly will come to tell the rector or vestry about it. A
deeper awareness of the ethical significance of business decisions,
a greater patience with one's children, a gift sent off to the
Presiding Bishop's Fund for World Relief can take place very
quietly and without measurable impact on the parish. The fruit
of the Spirit may be hidden or ripen slowly or have delayed
consequences. But where spiritual growth is occurring, the
measurable things will probably happen as well. The vestry can
establish goals and objectives in this area—and should, or else it
will be too easy to concentrate energy elsewhere, to the detri-
ment of parish life. Spiritual growth is less likely to occur in a
parish whose vestry members have given it no priority, assuming
it is an area beyond their purview or too difficult to analyze.

Goals and objectives can be set. The vestry can make it clear
by its own actions that these goals have priority. As vestry
members take part in prayer groups, attend church regularly,
participate in Bible study, and learn to articulate their faith more
easily, the fruit will grow. Then all the other goals and objectives
will fall into place and be supported and nourished by the renewal
of spiritual life.

Evangelism, Church Growth, Membership

This section has been given several titles because Episcopalians are often nervous about the word "evangelism." They equate it, unfortunately, with preaching on street corners, unsophisticated music, and pushing one's religion on others at inappropriate times—for example, on weekdays. This is too bad.

"Evangelism" comes from two Greek words meaning "good news." If we have a church we care about, that's good news, and we need to get the word around. But that doesn't necessarily mean trying to convert strangers at cocktail parties.

In the first place, those who have studied the subject will tell you that we all have different gifts. Some people have a talent for law or music; others (and sometimes the same people) have a talent for evangelism. Some studies suggest that those who have that talent may be less than 10 percent of all Christians. So relax; evangelism may not be your gift anyway.

But in another sense, evangelism is everybody's business whether they have a talent for it or not. We cannot simply say, "That's not my gift," and leave it to someone else. We are all part of a church that is called to do evangelism, and we can all contribute to the evangelistic work of the church even if our contribution is cooking the meals at which newcomers are welcomed or keeping the financial records without which the church doors could not be kept open for newcomers to enter.

Call the committee what you will—don't alarm people—but see that someone is charged with the business of helping people join your church. Look for one or two of the "natural evangelists" in your parish: the people who seem to have a knack for bringing others to church with them. Put them on the committee. Someone else may have better organizational talents and can chair the committee. Others will have the ideas and support skills needed. Let the committee meet monthly at least to review lists of newcomers, see that they are finding a place in parish life, organize welcoming teas or brunches or parties of some sort, and do the many other things that can be done to make the parish a welcoming place.

An effective membership committee will have an agenda as broad as the parish. Everything that happens in the parish has its impact on church growth. The committee will need liaison with the property committee, the worship committee, the Christian education committee, and even the budget committee.

Nothing else can be done well without money; how can evangelism? At the very least, there should be funds available for
literature and to attend conferences. Perhaps the committee will
need funds also for printing and mailings, to bring in speakers,
and even to put on special parish programs.

Perhaps after considering specific lists of newcomers and being
assured that they are being welcomed, the committee could take
the vestry committee list as its agenda. At one meeting it could
review the property from the point of view of church growth.
Is it well maintained and attractive? Is the lighting adequate? Is
the church warm enough? Are bathrooms clearly marked and
easily available? Is there adequate handicapped access? All these
and many similar questions are the concern of the membership
committee as well as the property committee. What about the
ushers committee? One grim usher can undo much good. What
about worship? Are the programs easy to follow, the hymns
singable, the choir eager for new members?

This is not to suggest that the membership committee should
constitute itself a super committee to which all others should
defer. Much tact will be needed to make the changes the
committee may deem desirable and not everything can be
changed—or should be. But church growth is legitimately everyone's concern and an active membership committee can and
should raise the consciousness level of the whole parish—in a
nice way!

Finally, be sure that the committee and its members take time
regularly for Bible study and prayer. What matters most is not
simply assembling the talent and energy but guiding and releasing
that energy through prayer. "I have planted," St. Paul wrote,
"and Apollos watered, but God gave the increase."

Working for Change

Churches—including Episcopal churches—have a reputation for
resisting change. A church whose clergy tend to vest themselves
in the garb of the Middle Ages and the Roman Empire does not
create an immediate image of open-mindedness and readiness to
accept new ideas. Yet in other ways the church is surprisingly
receptive to new ideas and is often torn between apostles of new
ideas and advocates of the status quo. Perhaps the (relatively!)
unchanging liturgy frees some individuals to make changes
elsewhere while in others it reinforces a disposition to keep
everything the same.

Newly elected vestry members may see themselves in both roles. They may be elected specifically because they have become known in the parish as effective change agents and even because they are known to be interested in working for change and growth in a particular area of parish life. Others may have been elected for their known devotion to tradition. But that, too, may involve changing attitudes. And how do you move an institution such as the church? Vestry members don't wear vestments to meetings—or even striped pants and cutaways—but, even in a year or two, vestry members can become more comfortable with things as they are and ready to explain to new members "how it's always been done."

If, however, there are new members with a vision—and if the annual vestry retreat or conference has given the whole vestry a vision—how can they work to accomplish it?

The first law of change is *participate*. Vestry members are participants, almost by definition. They are elected because they have been involved in parish activities. But more is needed. Participation on the vestry makes its own demands. Regular attendance is a *sine qua non*. Those who care must be present—or should put off serving on the vestry until they can be. Those who are present at vestry meetings and committee meetings, who are in church each Sunday, who stay and talk to others at the coffee hour, and who come to the covered-dish suppers and special events will be more effective than those who don't. And effecting change doesn't require lobbying people and twisting arms. Those who participate and work hard will find that their views will just naturally be listened to and respected. Other members will hesitate to overrule even the most eccentric views if the holder of them participates. It's almost that simple.

The second law of change is *involve others*. Very few people can do it alone. Even fewer can do it alone successfully. A parish is a corporate entity and, as such, has an amazing ability to absorb a variety of strong views without being much changed as a result. Corporate entities exist to give stability and continuity in the central issues of human life. Lacking that, they would constantly disintegrate and need to be replaced.

Therefore real change takes place only gradually and as large numbers become convinced of the value of change. Short-lived programs come and go as individuals generate enthusiasm and burn out. Those who have an enduring vision to share will work patiently to enlist others so that the work will not depend on their energy alone.

The third law of change is *take responsibility.* Hardly a Sunday goes by on which one member doesn't say to another—or to the rector—"Why doesn't somebody do X or Y or Z?" A frequently heard variation is, "Why don't *they* do X or Y or Z?" The answer is that "somebody" is "nobody" and that "they" is "we." Asking such questions accomplishes very little except to increase the risk of frustration: "I've asked about that again and again, but nothing ever seems to happen." There is a classic story of the usher who told the rector about a burned out light bulb in the side aisle five weeks in a row. On the sixth Sunday he changed it himself.

Most of us see things that need doing, but few of us are sufficiently motivated to do them ourselves. If, then, the problem is a low priority for us, we should not be surprised to find that it is a low priority for others. But if it seems important to us, it may be that the Holy Spirit is nudging us to do something about it ourselves.

Vestry members are uniquely well placed to get things done. They are almost always people who are involved. They are able to discuss with other vestry members what committee could appropriately be asked to take responsibility. And if there is no appropriate committee willing to tackle the issue, they can volunteer to head up an ad hoc committee themselves. Volunteers are seldom turned down.

Getting things done in a parish involves understanding structures and personalities, willingness to work, and a bit of psychology. Everything goes better for those vestry members who informally discuss their ideas with others, are prepared to work themselves, and know how to compromise when necessary.

Pray that the same Holy Spirit nudging you to get something done will nudge others also and give you the gifts needed to persuade and enlist those who can help to accomplish the task.

"Burnout"

"Burnout" is a currently fashionable word that can be used to describe several different phenomena. Whatever the terminology, it is a fact that service on the vestry sometimes leaves church members with more feelings of frustration than of accomplishment. Indeed, even those who have accomplished much can end their vestry experience with honors and recognition and still find themselves feeling "burned out," vaguely dissatisfied, and empty. Those who serve on vestries can contribute something special by being aware of the phenomenon and working to avoid it or overcome it in themselves and others.

"Type A" Burnout

The first type of "burnout" may be diagnosed as simple frustration. Members are elected as a recognition of accomplishment and begin their service with high hopes. Somehow the hopes are not fulfilled. Perhaps the member is assigned to the wrong committee or doesn't find the right slot. Perhaps whatever skills led to vestry election are not the skills needed on the vestry. Whatever the particular form the problem takes, all too often the result is a disillusioned church member.

"Type B" Burnout

The second type of burnout occurs when a member completes an extended term of service on the vestry in which much has been achieved. Perhaps the member has been a warden for several years and has been at the center of parish life. Yet a short time later this member, too, seems to be on the sidelines, perhaps no longer even attending church regularly.

The problem here is not so much exhaustion as disengagement. After an intense period of activity there is sudden calm, and all too easily comes a feeling that one is no longer needed or appreciated. Those who now occupy positions of leadership and activity can easily assume that there is no reason to worry about a former warden and not notice how that person is gradually drifting away.

Remedies

The simple remedy is attentiveness to the human beings with whom we work. Vestry members and clergy, in particular, need to be sensitive to others, help them find roles to play that are appropriate, and, if that is not possible, at least let them know that they are valued.

Former wardens and vestry members can be kept on the mailing list to receive minutes of meetings, asked to serve on appropriate committees, invited to an annual dinner of former wardens, or whatever seems appropriate. But, whatever you do, be aware; there is nothing more sad than the sight of a talented and concerned individual drifting away in frustration when something could be done to prevent it.

CHAPTER 9

The Search Process—
And Afterwards

The search for a new rector—or vicar or curate or other staff member—has evolved rapidly in recent years from an ad hoc process, dependent largely on the bishop's advice and the vestry members' personal contacts, into a carefully designed screening process employing computers and consultants and involving the whole parish to some degree. It can be a difficult, lengthy, time-consuming process, but it has its own very real rewards. Those involved in it will be given a liberal education and an often exhilarating, even inspiring exposure to the breadth and variety and strength of the church and its ordained ministry. They will be given also a new and deeper understanding of the unique character of their own parish. The final, most significant reward will be the celebration of a new ministry well chosen to lead the parish to new strength and new achievement.

Informing the Bishop

When a vacancy occurs, the bishop must be informed immediately and kept informed throughout. There are two reasons for this. First, the bishop is the "chief priest and pastor of a diocese" (*Book of Common Prayer* p. 855) and in that capacity is responsible for seeing that the ministry is properly carried out in each parish. Normally, the bishop or a deputy will consult with the vestry about providing ministry in the interim between rectors. Second, a priest is called not only to minister in a parish but also to take part in the corporate life of the diocese. The rector will probably serve on diocesan committees and work with the bishop and other clergy in a shared ministry. Thus the bishop has a vital interest in each parish's choice of clergy and must be given opportunity to "advise and consent."

The Interim

Although each bishop and diocese will have a somewhat different process that the vestry must follow, there is a generally agreed pattern. In the first place, most dioceses see value in an interim period of several months. This is not simply to allow time to search for a new rector—in many cases that could have been done before the former rector left—but, more importantly, to allow the new rector to come in after a breathing space and following an interim rector rather than a long-term predecessor. The relationship between priest and parish is very deep and the ending of that relationship is not unlike a death or divorce. The parish needs time to absorb the separation so that the new rector does not come into a parish still mourning its loss.

An interim rector can absorb some of the emotional burden and move on when the parish is ready to look forward again. The new rector can thus begin with less of the burden of comparison with the past. There are priests, many of them recently retired from parish ministry, who have become specialists in interim ministry and who can be extremely helpful in guiding a parish through a difficult transition.

The Search Process

The bishop and diocesan staff will ordinarily provide guidance in organizing and carrying out the search process. Published materials are available from the Church Deployment Office and other sources (see Appendix 6). The following notes are not intended to be complete, and the recommended process will vary from one diocese to another.

Form a Search Committee

The search committee, formed by the vestry and reporting to the vestry, should be chosen both to represent a cross section of the parish and also to carry out particular assignments. The self-study discussed below, for example, might be delegated to a special subcommittee, but the committee will need the skills to carry out this project and others either within its membership or available to it.

The search committee should include some vestry members but should not be primarily made up of vestry. The vestry will have all its usual work to do and, in the absence of a rector, even more. It would be difficult, if not impossible, to maintain its own work load and carry out a search as well.

Conduct a Self-Study

Probably the first assignment of the search committee (or a subcommittee assigned the task) will be to conduct a self-study and assemble a "parish profile." This study should deal with the surrounding community as well as with the parish, and it will be for the information not only of the committee and the candidates but also for the vestry and the entire parish.

Parishioners can easily assume that they know the parish and its situation. But do they know what percentage of the parish is over 70? Do they know the average income of the community? Do they know whether other parishioners value preaching, music, Christian education, or community outreach most? Everyone will have certain assumptions, but a careful self-study will provide answers that may be surprising. The clarification of parish characteristics and priorities will provide important guidance in defining the skills needed in a new rector or assistant.

Candidates also need this information. Committees have been known to take it for granted that all candidates are eager to come and need no particular information about the parish except, perhaps, the salary offered. In fact, some candidates may be quite unwilling to consider moving unless they see a clear challenge that they feel equipped to meet. Clergy have also been known to accept calls on the basis of information provided by one or two articulate members of a search committee only to learn later—too late—that the information, however well intentioned and sincerely believed by the informants, was quite inaccurate and that they do not really fit in the place to which they have moved with such high hopes and expectations.

A carefully researched, compiled, and printed self-study or parish profile is an invaluable asset in the search process and afterwards.

Define the Qualities Needed

The parish profile is helpful in moving to the next stage of the process and producing a candidate profile that fits that of the parish. It will provide information about the concerns of the parish, and those concerns for home visiting, preaching, youth ministry, social ministry, and the like will indicate the skills the parish feels the new rector will need. The Church Deployment Office will provide, directly or through the diocesan deployment officer, the forms that the search committee will need to complete for its own guidance and that of the bishop and the deployment office.

Assemble Resumes

Now comes the correspondence phase! Even before a parish profile and a search request are filed with the Church Deployment Office it is likely that the search committee will begin receiving resumes. Word gets around! Names of prospective candidates will come from the Church Deployment Office, the bishop, members of the parish, and (unsolicited) from candidates themselves. There was a time when it was considered "bad form" for clergy to indicate interest in moving. That time is past. The creation of the Church Deployment Office has, in effect, democratized the placement process. Those who are uncomfortable with the idea of clergy sending in resumes might consider whether they would be more comfortable with being dependent on the "old boy network" and the uncertainties of "who do you know?"

The committee should establish as early as possible what information it would like from each candidate. Typical requests are a resume, a Church Deployment Office (CDO) profile, several references, and, perhaps, a letter responding to specific questions. It is reasonable to ask candidates to provide this material by a specific date. In order to make comparisons fairly, the committee should have the same material from each candidate.

All resumes should be briefly acknowledged. If possible, the response should give some indication of the committee's schedule and when the prospective candidate might hear further. The search committee by this time should have a rough idea of how much time it will need for each step of the process and should, in fairness, keep candidates informed of its schedule and its progress.

Screen Resumes

Paperwork is unavoidable. The parish copier will be strained by the need to make copies of resumes and profiles so that all the material received can be available to as many members of the committee as necessary.

Guidance from the diocese or a consultant may help in reducing the pile of resumes to a manageable number. One obvious first step would be to assign each resume to two or three committee members and eliminate those that do not receive at least one positive response. Further screening by larger numbers of committee members can begin to establish a preliminary ranking so that a limited group can be chosen for visits or interviews.

Visits and Interviews

Before proceeding to visits and interviews, it is vital again to have the bishop's approval. The diocese may also provide guidance as to whether visits to other parishes should come first or whether candidates should be interviewed first and visited second. Both procedures have value.

Visits to other parishes provide the opportunity to see the candidate in his or her own environment. Most clergy preach better in their own community. They are preaching to people they know and care about, and that makes a difference. It is probably best to notify the candidate that a visit is planned. Committees sometimes find that the priest they have come to hear is not interested in moving or is not preaching on the Sunday the committee arrives. The "surprise" element is probably a negative, on balance. Besides, a planned visit may include a first interview and an opportunity to meet the candidate's family if arrangements are made in advance.

An interview in the searching parish has a different value. For one thing, it provides the candidate an opportunity to see the church that is conducting the search. For another, it provides opportunity for the full committee to meet the candidate. If the list of candidates has been narrowed to ten or fewer, the invitation to an interview should provide opportunity for the candidate to be given a tour of the community and to meet parish staff and leadership. If the candidate comes from another diocese, it may also be important to provide an opportunity for the candidate to meet the bishop.

Decision and Implementation

Every final decision in a search process (as in a marriage) involves generous elements of the unknown. The search committee's recommendation and the vestry's decision should focus as clearly as possible on the criteria established at the outset. What skills was the parish looking for and have they really been found? If the parish was looking for someone concerned for people, someone warm and outgoing may seem so at first meeting but in fact may be relatively insensitive to the needs of others. If the parish was looking for a teacher, scholarly credentials are not the same as an ability to communicate. It is easy to make a decision on the basis of personalities rather than skills. Never is prayer for guidance more important than at this point, but if prayer has been a vital part of the process from the beginning, it will be natural to rely on prayer here also to guide the final discussions and decision.

When a decision is made, it is usually advisable to notify the bishop first and then the candidate. Then, assuming both are agreed, move on to negotiate compensation terms and moving arrangements. Don't forget to notify other candidates and thank them for their participation in the process; they have contributed substantial amounts of time and energy and have almost certainly helped the parish clarify its goals and arrive at its final choice.

A New Beginning

New rectors have a reputation for "changing everything." But, of course, if nothing needs changing, the old rector—even dead—could probably continue to satisfy.

A new rector, inevitably, has a new outlook. He or she comes from a different place and has worked with different people and learned from different teachers. Some of these differences are what led the search committee and vestry to make the selection they did. They saw some differences that they hoped might make a difference in the parish. Of course, they were unaware of other differences in style and outlook, and some of these may take some getting used to. Usually it's worth the effort.

A new rector will see things that need doing—and will probably do them. The old rector may also have seen the need but knew people better and knew that to do certain things would upset certain people. So certain things remained undone. A new rector —blissfully ignorant of which toes are sensitive—will move ahead. Often the toes will turn out to be less sensitive than the former rector may have feared. Or perhaps the new rector has a certain charm—at first—that the former rector lacked or had lost. So the change is made more easily than might have been expected. Sometimes, of course, sensitive toes will be stepped on. Perhaps someone will leave in anger. But if the change was good, others will come into the parish as a result.

Remember, too, that there is change required on both sides. The parish will be aware only of the change asked of them, but the new rector may be changing even more, adapting the habits of a former parish to the very different customs, personalities, and requirements of a very different community. There is pain on both sides and, ideally, real growth on both sides as well.

Given time, new rectors also become aware of who cares about what and who will be upset at which change. The not-quite-so-new rector will also complete the immediate agenda and settle in for the longer haul. The pace of change will diminish—and that is a mixed blessing. The new rector gradually loses the new outlook and becomes sensitive to vested interests—and less able and willing to work effectively for change. The parish will settle again into a comfortable pattern, take many things for granted, develop bad habits, and become needful once more of the new insights and uncomfortable changes—the growing pains—that only a new rector can bring.

There will, of course, be a "honeymoon" during which rector and parish will be charmed with each other and accept much change with enthusiasm. It will pass, but take full advantage of it while it lasts. A sensitive vestry can play a vital role in helping the priest and parish to understand each other and move through the honeymoon into a strong and lasting relationship.

CHAPTER 10

The Diocese and the National Church

Church Government

An episcopal church, according to one standard dictionary, is a church "governed by bishops." The Episcopal church in the United States, however, is not "governed by bishops" but instead has a mixed type of government in which bishops, priests, and lay people all participate.

There are three traditional forms of church government: episcopal, presbyterial, and congregational. The Episcopal church's system contains elements of all three. Vestries function as a sort of board of "elders" (the literal meaning of "presbyter"), and congregations have a surprising degree of independence and ability to control their own affairs.

Bishops in the Episcopal church are often thought to have significant power, perhaps because their vestments are so impressive. In fact, however, their canonical or legal power is very limited, and they exercise authority in large part by better means than legal coercion: by example, exhortation, and personal leadership. This kind of authority was the only kind available to the first apostles, and it shifts the focus from "government" to "ministry." It is through their ministry, primarily, that bishops in the Episcopal church exercise leadership and make their influence felt.

The "episcopal" nature of the church, therefore, is very real. Most Episcopalians will always remember the moment when a particular bishop placed hands on their head as one of the most significant in their lives. And so it was, for they not only received gifts of the Spirit but also were linked through the bishop to a worldwide and age-old church and to the church of the apostles themselves.

Episcopalians are members not, primarily, of a local parish but of a worldwide church. They can visit another parish of the

Anglican communion, find a familiar liturgy (with infinite local variations!), and receive communion as a matter of course. If they are moving to a new community, they will be able to take a "letter of transfer" and have it accepted in their new parish to transfer their membership. But they need not, as members of congregational churches must, make a new profession of faith and be received again as church members in each new community.

Origins of the Episcopal Church's Government

The particular form of government that exists in the Episcopal church is an historical accident (God works through historical "accidents") and a result of the particular events that took place in this country before and immediately after the Revolutionary War. Although an Anglican priest came to Jamestown in 1607 as part of the first permanent settlement in this country and although the Church of England was planted in every colony in some form, there were no bishops in North America before the Revolution. Thus, Anglicanism developed here without its most characteristic form of ministry and the roles of priests and lay people expanded significantly as a result.

At the time of the Revolution, the Church of England was the established church in Virginia and other southern colonies, but the administration of the church was primarily in the hands of lay people: vestries in each parish and the colonial legislature in each colony. In New England, on the other hand, the Church of England existed as a tolerated minority, deeply aware of the things that distinguished it from the established Congregational church. New England Anglicans valued bishops but had never seen one. They saw them in theological terms and in their sacramental significance rather than as administrators and executives.

The constitution adopted for the church when the war was over, therefore, established a place for bishops with very limited powers. Through the first years of the church's life, bishops were usually rectors of large parishes who visited other parishes on occasion to confirm and who presided at an annual convention at which priests and lay people decided the issues before them.

The present pattern of church life has evolved gradually over the two centuries since, and the evolutionary process still continues. In response to particular challenges and in an effort to provide stronger leadership, individual bishops from time to time attempt to extend their control over diocesan institutions and parishes. Other bishops work to create new patterns of ministry by delegating administrative functions and freeing themselves for pastoral work and missionary leadership. These experiments, as they succeed or fail and are copied or abandoned, will gradually modify further the meaning of episcopacy and the shape of the church's life.

Parish and Diocese

The government of the Episcopal church may not be exclusively in the hands of bishops, but the diocese, not the parish, is nevertheless the basic unit of the church's life. No parish, however large, can represent the fullness and diversity of the church, its ecumenicity and catholicity, as adequately as the smallest diocese. No parish meeting, however large and diverse the parish may be, can represent the unity and variety of the Body of Christ as effectively as a diocesan gathering in which the laity and priests of scattered parishes are brought together around their bishop. Only as parishes are joined together over a wider area can their collective resources be focused on the points of special need and missionary opportunity. Without the unity of the diocese, the wealth of stronger parishes could be corrupting and the poverty of weaker parishes could be defeating. The corporate life of the diocese gives the church the balanced strength it needs to carry out its mission.

There are two central events on which the relationship between parish and diocese is based: the bishop's visitation and the diocesan convention. Of course, the bishop may visit a parish more than once a year, and there may be more than one convention annually. But the bishop's movement around the diocese creates one kind of unity, and the gathering of the parishes in convention creates another. The vestry is deeply involved in both.

The bishop's visit to the parish should not be seen simply as a confirmation visit. The confirmation and reception of new members is important, but the bishop comes primarily to visit the whole parish, to preside at the eucharist, and to preach the gospel. Only on Sundays when the bishop is present can the parish witness and participate in the normal pattern of liturgy; all other Sundays are abnormal.

The canons provide that the bishop should inspect the parish records (III, 15, Sec. 2[d]) but, more significantly, the bishop will want to hear from parishioners how their common life is going. Whether the bishop talks briefly with vestry members at the church door or at more length in a formal meeting, their perspective on parish life will help the bishop understand better this particular member of the diocesan body. Vestry members should make it a priority to be in church and to speak with the bishop when he visits.

Of equal importance is the vestry's participation in diocesan conventions. The canons of the church will establish the number of lay delegates each parish sends, but the vestry (or annual meeting) will select these delegates, and the vestry should expect a report from the parish delegates, whether or not they are vestry members, when the convention is over. It is the diocesan convention that makes the decisions that shape diocesan life and that directly affect every parish in it. The convention adopts the diocesan budget and establishes the process by which it is funded by the parishes. The convention may also adopt standards of clergy compensation. Such actions, of course, have a direct impact on the parish budget. The convention may also adopt resolutions on abortion and drugs and other national and international issues in an attempt to bring a Christian influence to bear not only on parishes but on society as a whole.

What some vestries never really understand is that the decisions made at the convention are usually only the last stage of a process that has been developing for months beforehand. The budget is shaped by a special committee that may have been working all year long, and it will probably be approved by diocesan council before it is presented to convention. And even though the convention delegates approve the budget, there is probably a committee that will oversee its implementation and, with the consent of the council, may reduce or increase expenditures where circumstances make it possible or necessary.

In the same way, resolutions are usually shaped and presented as a result of the work of other committees and regional groups of parishes.

In all this, the vestry can play a larger and more effective role if it is fully aware of the process and takes a full part in it throughout the year.

The National Church

Since the diocese is the basic unit of the church, the primary role of a "national church" is to coordinate the work of the individual dioceses and enable them to carry out appropriate projects together. In its secondary role, the national church establishes policy in such areas as marriage and divorce, standards for ordination, and procedures for the election of bishops. The General Convention, in its meetings every three years, makes the basic decisions on budget and policy and then leaves to the executive council of the church the work of carrying out the decisions made and dealing with issues that arise between conventions.

The presiding bishop is elected by General Convention and presides at meetings of the House of Bishops and the executive council. In the early days of the church, the presiding bishop was simply the senior bishop present (William White, the first presiding bishop, served for over forty years). But as the church grew and demands on the presiding bishop increased, it became obvious that some other system was needed. The present system was adopted in 1919. The presiding bishop serves as chief pastor to the other bishops and oversees the administrative work carried on by the staff of the executive council.

The executive council consists of bishops, priests, and lay people elected by the General Convention and by the provinces (nine regional groups of dioceses). The council meets at regular intervals to deal with policy matters that arise between conventions. The executive council staff serves as a resource to the church and carries out the decisions made by the Convention and council.

The National Church and the Parish

Although the primary role of the national church is in relation to dioceses, it does make an impact on the parish in a number of important ways.

In the first place, the budget of the national church is supported by the diocesan budget and normally requires from 20 percent to 30 percent of diocesan income. Thus, about a quarter of the money the parish sends to the diocese is sent on to the national church. The largest part of that budget is used for missionary work within the United States and overseas. Through its support of the diocese, the parish is contributing significantly to the church's national and worldwide mission.

Most parishes also make some direct contribution each year to outreach on a national and international level. The Good Friday offering is usually designated for the work of the church in the Holy Land. The church school Lenten offering is ordinarily designated for mission work. And the Presiding Bishop's Fund for World Relief gives help to victims of hunger and disaster wherever they may be. All these offerings are coordinated by departments of the executive council.

One of the most important departments of the executive council for local parishes and vestries is the Church Deployment Office. The "CDO" maintains a computer listing of all the clergy of the Episcopal church with information concerning their experience and special skills. It is an important resource (discussed in more detail in chapter nine) for parishes needing a new rector, curate, or other assistant.

Other important work carried out by the executive council staff is the development of materials for stewardship and Christian education and the coordination of special ministries.

In Conclusion

If it has not been said already, it should be said in closing: no single person can be an expert in every area of vestry responsibility. And even an expert on insurance or building maintenance cannot be sure of properly weighing church needs in that area against the church's mission of evangelism and service. Vestry members must learn to work together, to listen to each other, and attempt to balance competing needs and priorities with patience, understanding, and a certain sense of humor. If the church could survive in the catacombs, it can probably survive in our communities. If it could survive "dungeon, fire, and sword" (Hymn 558), it can also survive mistaken priorities and flawed committee work.

A word frequently used in these pages is "leadership." Another important word is "discipleship." Christian leaders are, first of all, followers; they are able to lead others because they themselves have a leader. Charismatic leaders are often able to lead large numbers of people by sheer force of personality, and history is littered with the resultant wreckage. Leadership that begins with discipleship, on the other hand, need not be dramatic or even obvious. But what it accomplishes, quietly, faithfully, and persistently, is far more lasting and valid.

The man or woman who agrees to serve on a vestry takes on a job that, to be well done, must claim priority in time and energy. It cannot be just "one more committee." But if it is given the time it requires and if it is grounded in prayer and a spirit of discipleship, it can change your life.

Appendices

Appendix 1

Summary of Relevant Canons

Note: these summaries are too brief to be relied on for legal guidance. They are intended only to give general guidance and to indicate which canons may be relevant in a particular situation.

Concerning Buildings and Property

I, 7, Sec. 4. No vestry may alienate (sell or mortgage) church property without the consent of the bishop and standing committee.

III, 15, Sec. 1(c). The rector is given "use and control of the Church and Parish buildings" to carry out the work of the ministry.

Concerning Finances

I, 6, Sec. 1. An annual report is required on parish receipts, expenditures, and property held.

I, 7, Sec. 1. This canon ("Of Business Methods in Church Affairs") requires that trust funds be properly deposited and recorded, that treasurers be bonded, that accounts be properly recorded and audited, that buildings and property be adequately insured, and that the fiscal year begin on January 1.

III, 15, Sec. 2(e). The undesignated offering at the service of Holy Communion one Sunday each month shall be given to the rector for charitable purposes.

Vestry Responsibilities

I, 6, Sec. 1. The annual report of membership and finances is the joint responsibility of the vestry and rector.

III, 5, Sec. 4. The vestry must certify its opinion of the qualifications of a church member applying to be a postulant (first step candidate) for ordination.

III, 6, Sec. 2(c). The above certification must be reaffirmed before the member becomes a candidate (second step).

III, 9, Sec. 5(4). The vestry must certify the above candidate before ordination as a deacon.

III, 10, Sec. 4(3). The vestry must certify the candidate before ordination to the priesthood.

III, 15, Sec. 1(b). Vestry approval must be given to the selection of assistant clergy.

III, 15, Sec. 2(d). Vestry and clergy are both responsible for showing the bishop the parish register at the annual visitation and for reporting on the state of the parish.

III, 15, Sec. 4(b). The vestry is to notify the bishop if the rector is unable or unwilling to perform services. They must also give consent to the choice of an interim Minister.

III, 18, Sec. 1-4. Lists requirements for the calling of a rector.

III, 19, Sec. 1. The vestry must give consent to the resignation of a rector.

Other Matters

I, 17. This canon defines church membership. A "communicant in good standing" is a baptized person who has received Holy Communion in this church at least three times in the preceding year and who has been faithful in working, praying, and giving for the spread of the Kingdom.

III, 19, Sec. 2. This canon describes the process for dissolving the pastoral relationships when there is a disagreement. The bishop with the standing committee is the "ultimate arbiter and judge."

Appendix 2

Sample Property Surveys

The following pages are designed as working documents and a permanent record for the Committee on Buildings and Grounds (by whatever name the committee is known). These pages can be duplicated on an office copier exactly as given or revised to fit particular local situations. No permission is required from the publisher.

Sample A. One copy of this page is needed for each building and is used to provide specific information about the roof and to note the condition of walls, windows, gutters, and leaders as well as security, safety, and access problems that need attention.

Sample B. One copy of this page may be useful to provide an index of the pages (Sample C) provided for each room and area within the building.

Sample C. One copy should be made for each room and area. In a building with numerous rooms and areas, these pages should be numbered consecutively and indexed on Sample page B.

Sample D. One copy of this page may be adequate but it may be necessary to provide more space for each category (lawns, trees, walls) depending on the circumstances of each church.

Building Survey A.   Date:_____

Name of Building: _____

Roof: Date installed _____

       Contractor_____

       Guaranteed for _____ years

       Present condition _____

       _____

Walls: East _____

      South_____

      West _____

      North _____

Windows: East_____

       _____

      South _____

      _____

      West _____

      _____

      North_____

      _____

Gutters and Leaders: _____

_____

Other: _____

_____

Doors:

Security Problems:

Safety Problems:

Handicapped Access:

Page: _____

Building Survey B.   Date: _____

Name of Building: _____

List of Rooms and Areas for Survey:

1._____ Survey page _____

2._____ Survey page _____

3._____ Survey page _____

4._____ Survey page _____

5._____ Survey page _____

6._____ Survey page _____

7._____ Survey page _____

8._____ Survey page _____

9._____ Survey page _____

10._____ Survey page _____

11._____ Survey page _____

12._____ Survey page _____

13._____ Survey page _____

14._____ Survey page _____

15._____ Survey page _____

16._____ Survey page _____

17._____ Survey page _____

18._____ Survey page _____

19._____ Survey page _____

20._____ Survey page _____

(One copy for each building)

Page: _____

Building Survey C.   Date: _____

Name of Building: _____

Name of Room or Area: _____ Floor: _____

Ceiling:

Walls

Windows:

Floor:

Lighting:

Furnishings:

Fire Safety:
  —fire extinguishers
  —fire doors
  —exit signs
  —alarms
  —smoke detectors

Routine Maintenance:

Major Repairs:

(One copy for each room or area)

Page: _____

Gounds Survey D.   Date: _____

    Routine Maintenance:

        Lawn mowing/leaf raking

        Trees

        Shrubbery

        Gardens

        Walls

        Sidewalks

        Parking Lot/s

    Major Improvements:

Appendix 3

Sample Statements of Purpose

"As a body of Christians, our mission is to worship and serve God by creating and sustaining a Spirit-filled community that enables all people to know and love Jesus Christ as Savior."

* * *

"The Mission of St. Mary's Episcopal Church is to be an outward and visible sign, sacrament and instrument, of the now living and risen Christ, guided by the Holy Spirit.

"As the sacrament of the living and risen Christ, its members accept the dual responsibility to seek continually to deepen their knowledge and faith in Christ and to share with each other and the community of Shelter Island and the community of the world, the ministry of Jesus Christ as each person received the gifts of the Holy Spirit."

* * *

"St. John's Episcopal Church is a family called by Christ
  —to grow spiritually
    —to share our life with others
      —and to make known his love through word and deed"

* * *

"St. Mark's is where the good news of freedom (to be human, to be right, to be wrong, from the law, to be judged) and forgiveness given by Jesus Christ is projected by the life of the community and, hopefully, heard. This is not something that can be told. Only through involvement can one appropriate it. This is not a prescription for one's life but an invitation to join.

"St. Mark's is a community whose purpose is to nurture and support its people in discovering who they are and where they are. Church is primarily a training camp (discovering with others where the battles are and equipping one for the fight) not an operating combat unit . . ."

* * *

"A community of Prayer—Peace—Passion"

Appendix 4

Sample Columbarium Contract[1]

AGREEMENT RELATING TO
THE COLUMBARIUM
IN THE CHURCHYARD OF

AGREEMENT made this . . . . . day of . . . ., 19 . . . . between . . . ., Party of the First Part, and THE RECTOR, WARDENS AND VESTRY OF . . . . CHURCH, of . . . . , Party of the Second Part:

WITNESSETH, that in consideration of the payment by Party of the First Part to the Party of the Second Part of the sum of $ . . . . (and the promise of the Party of the First Part to pay the additional amounts of $ . . . . . on . . . ., 19 . . . ., and $ . . . . . on . . . ., 19 . . . .) to be used for the general purposes of the Party of the Second Part in any manner which it desires, the Party of the Second Part hereby agrees to reserve and set aside for the Party of the First Part a { double single } Niche in the Columbarium of   Church, for the interment of the ashes of . . . . and . . . . subject to the terms and conditions set forth on the reverse side hereof which are hereby made a part of this agreement.

IN WITNESS WHEREOF, we have hereunto affixed our signatures as of the date and year above stated.

. . . .
Party of the First Part

_____ CHURCH

By . . . . *(Rector)*
Party of the Second Part

---

[1]Permission for reproduction hereby granted by Christ Church, Bronxville, New York.

TERMS AND CONDITIONS

1) Complete control of the Churchyard and all parts thereof shall be vested in the Party of the Second Part. The Party of the First Part does not acquire any property rights of any kind whatsoever in or to the Niche referred to in the annexed agreement.

2) The Party of the First Part may designate the ashes of such persons as he desires to have interred in the Niche referred to, but the Party of the Second Part shall have sole discretion as to the persons whose ashes may be interred therein and the permission of the Party of the Second Part must in each instance be obtained in writing prior to the placing of any ashes in such Niche. The right of interment hereby given to the Party of the First Part shall not be assigned or transferred without the written consent of the Party of the Second Part, nor shall the Party of the Second Part be obliged to recognize any right to interment hereunder in any heirs, distributees or devisees of the Party of the First Part. If the Party of the First Part desires to assign or transfer any right of interment hereby given, he shall submit the name or names of the assignee or transferree to the Party of the Second Part, which reserves the right to withhold consent to such assignment or transfer for any reason which it in its sole discretion shall deem proper. If consent is given to such assignment or transfer, or if the Party of the Second Part shall recognize any right of heirs, distributees or devisees of the Party of the First Part with respect to this agreement, or if the Party of the First Part shall make a designation as herein provided which is acceptable to the Party of the Second Part, the assignee, transferree, designee, heir or heirs, distributees or devisees shall be bound by all the terms and conditions hereof.

3) The type, size, shape and design of any urn containing ashes to be interred in such Niche shall be subject to the absolute control of the Party of the Second Part in all respects. No urn containing ashes placed in such Niche may be removed except by and with the consent of the Party of the Second Part first had and obtained and no right whatsoever shall exist in the heirs at law of the Party of the First Part, or anyone else, to have such ashes removed. In the event of removal, all rights to the space in such Niche shall cease and terminate, and any rights given hereunder shall revert to the Party of the Second Part. In the event that it shall be necessary at any time to change the location or discontinue the use of the Churchyard or any part thereof, the Party of the Second Part may in its discretion remove the urns in any Niche or Niches whose use is discontinued, and may place such urns in other suitable Niches as in its sole discretion the Party of the Second Part may deem fit and proper.

4) The material, size, shape and character of the marker or other designation for such Niche, and the legend and lettering thereon, shall be subject to the absolute control of the Party of the Second Part. The Party of the First Part shall be charged with the actual cost of such marker, designation, legend or lettering, and agrees to pay for the same upon the rendition of a statement therefor.

5) The Party of the Second Part agrees to exercise reasonable care in the maintenance of the Churchyard. No liability of any kind or character whatsoever is assumed by the Party of the Second Part for the maintenance or preservation of the ashes of any person interred in such Niche or for any loss or damage to the urns or ashes of any such deceased person, nor is any liability of any kind whatsoever assumed by the Party of the Second Part for any matter or thing relating to the Churchyard, its use or subsequent maintenance, except for failure to exercise reasonable care.

6) All services at which ashes are interred in the Churchyard shall be conducted by the Rector of Christ Church, Bronxville or by other clergy acting with his permission and under his direction. In case the parish be without a rector, services shall be conducted by clergy officiating in the parish by permission of the Vestry of Christ Church.

7) Flowers may be placed in the Churchyard only in such places as may, from time to time, be designated by the Party of the Second Part and may be removed at any time by like authority, and shall be at all times be subject to the control and regulations of the Party of the Second Part.

8) If for any reason such Niche is not used for the interment of the ashes of a deceased person as provided in the agreement attached hereto within a reasonable time after the death of such person, such reasonable time to be determined solely by the Party of the Second Part, such Niche shall be deemed to be abandoned by the Party of the First Part or his heirs, successors or assignees and shall revert to the sole use of the Party of the Second Part, and the Party of the Second Part shall be under no obligation whatsoever to return the contribution or any part thereof theretofore paid by the Party of the First Part to the Party of the Second Part.

9) In no event shall such Niche be used until the entire contribution has been paid by the Party of the First Part to the Party of the Second Part.

Appendix 5

A Glossary of Church Terms

Archdeacon: A priest (usually) who is given certain administrative responsibilities in a specific area of the diocese.

Archdeaconry: An administrative area of the diocese.

Canon: (1) A church law. (2) A priest on the staff of a cathedral (sometimes an honorary title).

Cathedral: The church in which the bishop has his "cathedra" or chair.

Coadjutor: An assistant bishop with specifically assigned areas of jurisdiction and the right of succession when the diocesan bishop retires or dies.

Columbarium: A place for the interment of ashes or cremated remains.

Curate: In the United States, a traditional title for assistant parish clergy.

Dean: (1) The priest in charge of a cathedral or seminary. (2) A priest assigned to assist the bishop administratively in a deanery.

Deanery: An administrative area within a diocese (an "archdeaconary," by another name.)

Diocese: The basic unit of the church; a group of parishes in one geographical area with a bishop as the chief minister.

Rector: The chief pastor in a self-supporting parish, instituted by the bishop.

Sexton: The custodian in a church or cathedral.

Suffragan: An assistant bishop without right of succession and (usually) without specifically designated areas of jurisdiction.

Verger: An official who carries a rod of office in church processions; since the sexton often acts in this capacity, the term is often used as a title for the sexton.

Vicar: In the United States, the priest in charge of a mission church or assisted parish. Ordinarily appointed by the bishop, not elected as is a rector.

Appendix 6
Resources

Institutions

The Alban Institute 4125 Nebraska Avenue Washington, DC 20016	"Resources for people who care about congregations," publications, training programs, consultation
The American Guild of Organists 815 Second Avenue New York, NY 10017	Sample contracts, job descriptions, and search assistance
Church Deployment Office 815 Second Avenue New York, NY 10017	Assistance in clergy placement, materials about the search process
Church Insurance Corporation Church Life Insurance Corporation 800 Second Avenue New York, NY 10017	Various types of insurance, brochures, and consultation
Church Pension Fund 800 Second Avenue New York, NY 10017	Information about the clergy pension plan
Consortium of Endowed Episcopal Parishes Suite 222, Guaranty Building 22 North Meridian Street Indianapolis, Indiana 46204	An organization to assist well-endowed parishes in their financial planning and charitable giving.
The Episcopal Church Building Fund 815 Second Avenue New York, NY 10017	Assistance in planning, financing, construction, improvement, and repair of parish buildings
Forward Movement Publications 412 Sycamore Street Cincinnati, OH 45202	Tracts and booklets on a variety of church subjects
Morehouse-Barlow Co. 78 Wilton Road Wilton, CT 06897	Church supplies and publications
Office for Ministry Development 815 Second Avenue New York, NY 10017	Sample "letters of agreement"
Stewardship Office Diocese of New York 1047 Amsterdam Avenue New York, NY 10025	Stewardship manual for parishes, curriculum for church schools

Books

Accessibility Guidelines for Episcopal Churches, available from
   the Task Force on Accessibility (815 Second Avenue, New
   York, NY 10017); one copy free, additional copies at $1 each.

New Models for Creative Giving, by Raymond Knudsen,
   Morehouse-Barlow, 1985. Provides information about
   electronic transfer systems of giving.

The Episcopal Church Annual, Morehouse-Barlow

A Manual of Accounting Principles and Reporting Practices,
   Executive Council of the Episcopal Church, 815 Second
   Avenue, New York, New York 10017

How to Care for Religious Properties, by Michael Lynch, available
   from the Preservation League of New York State, 307
   Hamilton Street, Albany, New York, 12210 ($2.00)

Index